HOME LIBRARY

SIMPLE
HOME
REPAIR

Contents

ISBN: 0-88176-380-2   Manufactured in the United States of America

Publications International, Ltd., has made every effort to ensure the accuracy and reliability of the information, instructions, and directions in this book; however, it is in no way to be construed as a guarantee, and Publications International, Ltd., is not liable in case of misinterpretation of the directions, human error, or typographical mistakes.

Illustrations: Clarence A. Moberg

Introduction

Are you troubled by a clogged toilet, mildew problems, broken windows, or squeaking floors? Would you like to be able to repair your broken doorbell or replace a wall outlet? Do you want to weather-strip your doors and windows, install a deadbolt lock, or paint, panel, or paper a room? You'll find out how to do all these tasks—plus many more—in SIMPLE HOME REPAIR.

Even if you've never done anything more difficult than changing a light bulb, SIMPLE HOME REPAIR will show you how to fix, maintain, and improve a number of things in and around your house. Simple, step-by-step instructions, a list of tools and materials required for each job, and clear illustrations guide you through more than fifty basic repairs you will soon master.

Section one covers fixing holes in concrete slabs, steps, and walls. You will also learn how to tuck-point loose mortar joints and replace a damaged brick.

The next section deals with fixing up the exterior of your home. There's no need to be troubled anymore by a leaky roof, gutter, or garden hose.

Following that are projects designed to aid you in replacing a broken window, mending a hole in a screen, and unsticking a door.

Homeowners will be especially interested in the section that includes tips to make your home more secure and how to install a new lock.

After that, SIMPLE HOME REPAIR will tell you how to

keep the interior of your house in tip-top shape. How to refinish a hardwood floor, lay a tile floor, and remove spots from resilient floors are just a few of the topics discussed. From there we move on to paneling walls, and the correct way to wallpaper a room.

Also included are hints to make interior and exterior painting a breeze. Special attention is paid to paintbrush care, which supplies you with enough tips to make your paintbrushes last virtually forever.

All homeowners are at one point or another bothered by a clogged drain or a faucet that won't stop dripping. After reading and understanding basic plumbing procedures you'll never be stymied by a leaky pipe again.

Following is a section dealing with basic electrical repairs. You will learn how to work on electrical devices (once the power has been cut off) and soon will master a wide variety of restorations that will save you time and money on costly repair bills.

The last section of the book covers furniture restoring. How to remove cigarette burns and spots are just a couple of the projects designed to help you remedy minor surface defects.

And that's the story of SIMPLE HOME REPAIR, a book we hope will become a valued friend of yours in the years—and projects—to come. Start working with it today, and take the first step toward putting your entire house in excellent condition.

1 Patching Surface Holes in a Concrete Slab

QUITE FREQUENTLY, the surface of a concrete drive, walk, or patio gets crumbly, and before long you notice some big holes. You would be wise to patch small holes before they become big problems. Most patches come out after a while, and then you're right back where you started. Do it right with the following method, however, and your patch will stay put.

HERE IS WHAT YOU WILL NEED

Materials	Tools
☐ Ready (sand) concrete mix	☐ Hammer
☐ Concrete bonding agent	☐ Chisel
☐ Tarp or plastic sheet	☐ Goggles
☐ Plastic coffee can lid	☐ Garden hose
☐ 2x4	☐ Paintbrush
	☐ Metal wheelbarrow
	☐ Trowel
	☐ Wooden float
	☐ Metal float
	☐ Push broom

1. With a hammer and chisel, remove every bit of loose concrete, then hose out the cavity until it is perfectly clean. When chipping concrete, always wear goggles to protect your eyes. In addition, cut an "X" in a plastic coffee can lid and slip it over the chisel to shield you from flying fragments.

2. Get a sack of ready mix (called a *sand mix*) and a small can of a bonding agent. The bonding agent is the key to creating a patch that is bonded permanently to the old concrete. You can buy patching mix that includes a bonding agent, but if you are patching many holes, the cost of the mix might be prohibitive.

3. Remove any standing water in the hole.

4. Brush on the bonding agent, following manufacturer's directions.

5. Prepare the sand mix according to directions. Make sure that each grain of sand is coated with the gray mix, using only the prescribed amount of water. A watery mix may be easier to work with, but it loses much of its strength. A metal wheelbarrow makes an ideal container for mixing.

6. Pour the mix into the hole, and then use a trowel to poke it in place completely.

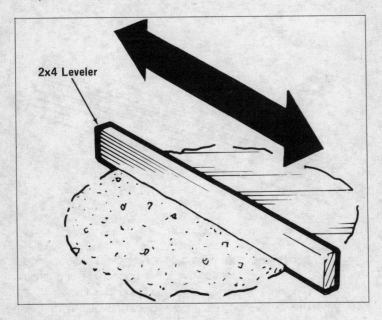

2x4 Leveler

7. Pull a 2x4 across the top to level the patch.

8. When the water sheen disappears, start to smooth the patch with a **wooden** float. You will soon see some water back on the surface; when you notice a sheen again, stop the smoothing process.

9. If additional smoothing is necessary, wait until the surface sheen goes away again, then smooth with a **metal** float. Re-

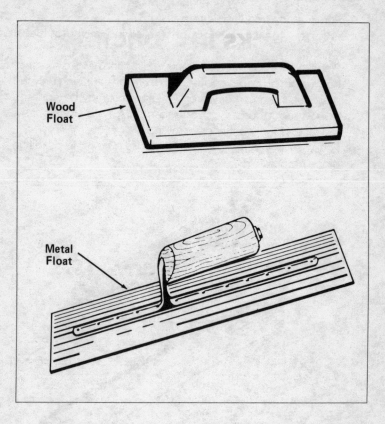

Wood Float

Metal Float

member, though, that most outdoor concrete projects should have a fairly rough finish for better traction. Pulling a push broom across the surface gives you this kind of finish.

10. When the water sheen disappears again, cover the patch with a tarp or a sheet of plastic.

11. Remove the tarp or plastic sheet every day and spray the concrete lightly with a fine mist from your garden hose. If possible, repeat this process for six days, re-covering the patch after each spraying. You are letting the concrete *cure.* Curing is very important since failure to do so permits the concrete to dry out too quickly, resulting in a new batch of holes to patch very soon.

Cracks in Concrete   2

CRACKS in concrete tend to grow. The small crack running across the patio today will become a chasm between two smaller patios in very short order. Moisture and temperature changes push at the sides of the crack as more of the surface inside comes loose. Patching can stop the crack's progress.

HERE IS WHAT YOU WILL NEED

Materials	Tools
☐ Portland cement or concrete bonding agent	☐ Cold chisel
	☐ Hammer
☐ Plastic coffee can lid	☐ Goggles
☐ Sand or gravel mix	☐ Stiff broom
☐ 2x4	☐ Garden hose
☐ Tarp sheet	☐ Small trowel or putty knife

1. Use a cold chisel to convert the crack to a groove that is at least an inch deep and ½ inch wide. When chipping concrete, always wear goggles to protect your eyes. In addition, cut an "X" in a plastic coffee can lid and slip it over the chisel to shield you from flying fragments.

2. Undercut the groove to make it wider at the bottom; undercutting helps lock in the patch.

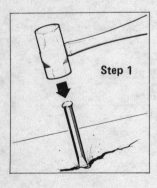

Step 1

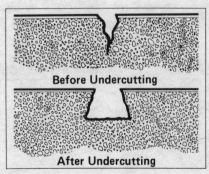

Before Undercutting

After Undercutting

3. Brush and wash out all the loose concrete with a stiff broom and strong spray from your garden hose. If the crack goes all the way through the slab, tamp in a sand base.
4. Leave all surfaces wet, but get rid of any standing water.
5. Coat all surfaces with a creamy mix of portland cement and water, or use a bonding agent.
6. Prepare either a stiff sand mix or one with small gravel.
7. Tamp the mix into the crack with a small trowel or putty knife.
8. When the new concrete begins to stiffen (usually about 45 minutes later), smooth it with a trowel or a 2x4. Cover with a tarp or plastic sheet.
9. Remove the tarp or plastic sheet every day and spray the concrete lightly with a fine mist from your garden hose. If possible, repeat this process for six days, re-covering the patch after each spraying. You are letting the concrete *cure*. Curing is very important since failure to do so permits the concrete to dry out too quickly, resulting in a new batch of holes to patch very soon.

3 Patching Concrete Steps

THE EDGES OF concrete steps receive a great deal of wear, and in most cases they can take it. Once edges start to fall apart, however, they keep on until there is not much left. Not only do crumbled steps look bad, they also pose a real safety hazard. Patching damaged concrete steps is a fairly easy repair. Here is all you do.

HERE IS WHAT YOU WILL NEED

Materials	Tools
☐ Wood planks	☐ Hammer
☐ Bricks	☐ Cold chisel
☐ 2x4	☐ Garden hose
☐ Nails	☐ Paintbrush

Materials	Tools
☐ Concrete bonding agent	☐ Trowel
☐ Ready-mixed concrete	☐ Wooden float
☐ Tarp or plastic sheet	

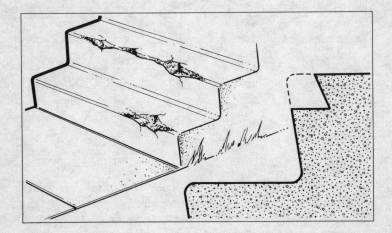

1. Undercut the crumbling edge with a hammer and cold chisel. Undercutting is the process of cutting a "V" back into the solid concrete so that the patch will have a better chance of locking in place.
2. Remove all loose concrete, and clean the area thoroughly with the strong spray of the garden hose.
3. Build a form by placing a board against the riser and securing it with several bricks; they should hold the board firmly in place. Select two planks that are wide enough and tall enough and place them against the two sides. Then angle a 2x4 as a brace, and nail it in place. Make sure that the top of your form is level with the step.
4. Paint the area to be covered with a concrete bonding agent, following the directions on the can. You can find concrete bonding agents at any hardware store.
5. Use ready-mixed concrete of the sand mix formula. Add no more

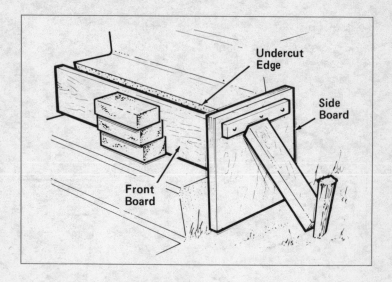

water than the directions specify, and mix completely until every grain of sand is coated with the cement.

6. Use a trowel to poke the concrete mix in place, and check to be sure that you leave no air spaces back in the "V."

7. Finish off the concrete patch so that it is level with the rest of the step. You can use your trowel or a wooden float to get the patch level.

8. Make the patch match the texture of the rest of the step, and then cover it with a tarp or a plastic sheet.

9. Remove the tarp or plastic sheet every day and spray the concrete lightly with a fine mist from your garden hose. If possible, repeat this process for six days, re-covering the patch after each sprinkling. You are letting the concrete *cure*. Curing is very important since failure to do so permits the concrete to dry out too quickly, resulting in a new batch of holes to patch very soon.

You can remove the forms as soon as the concrete patch sets up, but by leaving them in place during the curing process, you reduce the likelihood of someone accidentally stepping on the patch before it is fully cured.

Replacing a Brick 4

A LOOSE BRICK should be reattached and a damaged brick should be replaced. Just buy a sack of mortar mix and you are ready to go to work. After you mix up a batch of the mortar, you should be able to get the loose brick back in place before it falls out and creates an even bigger headache.

HERE IS WHAT YOU WILL NEED

Materials	Tools
☐ Mortar mix	☐ Hammer
☐ Mortar coloring	☐ Goggles
☐ Replacement brick	☐ Cold chisel
☐ Bucket	☐ Wire brush
☐ Plastic coffee can lid	☐ Garden hose
	☐ Trowel

1. Remove the mortar around the loose or damaged brick with a hammer and chisel. When chipping concrete, always wear safety goggles to protect your eyes. In addition, cut an "X" in a plastic coffee can lid and slip it over the chisel to shield you from flying fragments. If the brick is already damaged, you can use a chisel to break it up too. If the brick is just loose, though, be careful not to break it as you chip the mortar to get it out. You will want to use the brick again in a few minutes.
2. After the brick comes out, chip away all the mortar that is still clinging to it.
3. Drop the brick into a bucket of water.
4. Go back to the hole and chip away all remaining mortar. You may have to use a wire brush to get the hole really clean. When you get all the mortar out, hose down the cavity.
5. Mix the mortar, adding coloring to shade the mixture so that it matches the rest of the wall.
6. Lay a bed of mortar down on the damp floor of the hole where the brick will go.
7. Take the brick out of the bucket of water, but do not dry it; just

shake off any surface water. Spread the two ends and the top of the brick with mortar.

8. Insert the brick in the hole and press it in place, lining it up with the other bricks.

9. Use your trowel to force back into the cavity all the mortar that was pushed out when you inserted the brick.

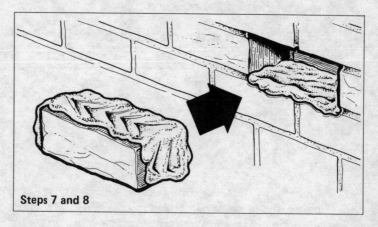

Steps 7 and 8

10. Clean away any excess mortar.

11. Now—before the mortar sets up—make the new joints match the old ones. Remember that mortar dries faster on a hot or windy day.

5 Tuck-Pointing Loose Mortar Joints

TUCK POINTING is removing old mortar between bricks and replacing it with new. Loose or crumbling mortar must be replaced or it will allow moisture to penetrate, and moisture can damage the interior wall. In addition, one loose brick tends to cause more crumbling and loose mortar outside. The next thing you know, you will have a whole wall of bad mortar joints to fix. Therefore, go ahead and fix them now, before the situation gets any worse. Just buy a sack of mortar mix that has everything already in it except the water, and your tuck pointing should be a snap.

HERE IS WHAT YOU WILL NEED

Materials	Tools
☐ Mortar mix	☐ Cold chisel
☐ Corrugated cardboard	☐ Hammer
☐ Mortar coloring	☐ Safety goggles
	☐ Garden hose
	☐ Trowel
	☐ Jointer tool or short piece of pipe
	☐ Stiff brush

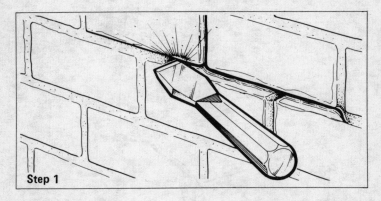

Step 1

1. Clean out the loose or crumbling joints with a cold chisel and hammer. Cut down to a depth of at least ½ inch, attacking the vertical joints first and then the horizontal ones. Be sure to wear safety goggles when chipping the mortar.
2. Turn the hose on the cleared joint to flush away all loose mortar and dust.
3. Now you are ready to mix the new mortar. You should know that

the mix will probably be an entirely different shade when it dries than when you first mix it. Mix a trial batch and apply it to a piece of corrugated cardboard. The porous cardboard will absorb most of the water, and the mortar that is left will be about the same shade it will be when dry. The next step is to add some color (available at hardware stores) to the mortar so that it will match the rest of the walls. When you arrive at a match on the cardboard, you will have a good idea of what the wet mix should look like to achieve the desired results.

4. Dampen the joints to be tuck-pointed.
5. Force mortar into the joints with a trowel, filling the vertical joints first and then the horizontals. Press the mortar into the new joints firmly to make certain that you leave no cavities.

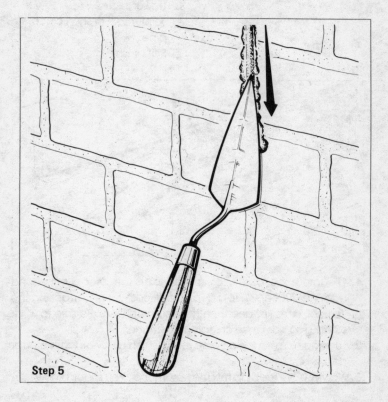

Step 5

6. Now—before the mortar sets up—you must make the new joints look the same as the old. On a hot or warm and windy day, the mortar will dry out quickly, so you must work fast. Scrape off the excess mortar before you start tuck-pointing, and then use a jointer tool or a trowel to achieve the desired effect.
7. After the mortar sets up, take a stiff brush and clean the face of the bricks.

Fixing a Leaky Garden Hose

6

MENDING a garden hose is easy if you have the right materials. A quick trip to the hardware store will help you get started.

HERE IS WHAT YOU WILL NEED

Materials	Tools
☐ Mending unit	☐ Knife
☐ Hose coupling	☐ Hammer
☐ Washer	☐ Screwdriver
	☐ Soldering iron

1. Cut out the section of the hose with the hole in it and take it to the hardware store. The hardware dealer will sell you a mending unit of the correct size for your hose. Although some mender manufacturers claim that their products can be used on both plastic and rubberized hoses, you should buy the one made especially for the type of hose you have.
2. The mender for a rubber hose has a short corrugated nipple or tube that you slip into each end of the cut hose.
3. When you get the tube snugged up all the way on both sides, place the mender on a wood block.
4. Take a hammer and start tapping the clawlike fingers on the

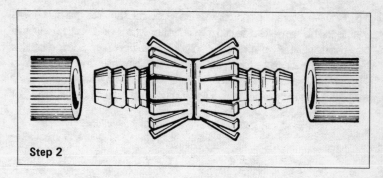

Step 2

flange of the mender down against the hose. When all of the prongs are resting securely against the hose, the leak is mended.

5. The mender for a plastic hose is a tube that fits inside with threaded screw clamps that go over the hose. As you tighten the clamps, the threads tighten into the hose and hold it against the tube. To make a plastic hose more pliable and easier to work with, hold the ends in very hot water before inserting the tube.

6. You can sometimes mend a tiny hole in a plastic hose by touching a hot soldering iron to the hole. The heat will melt some of the plastic and close the hole.

7. You can replace hose couplings, but before you replace a coupling because it leaks, check to be sure that the washer is all right. Even if the washer looks good, it may be compressed and not able to provide a tight seal. Therefore, try a new washer before you install a replacement coupling.

7 Repairing a Roof

ROOF LEAKS can do all sorts of damage inside your home. Fixing the leak is often an easy task, but—since leaks are very elusive—locating the leak can take forever. Water can enter at one point in your roof and follow a rafter for many feet before it drips down onto the ceiling. Sometimes a leak occurs only when the wind is blowing

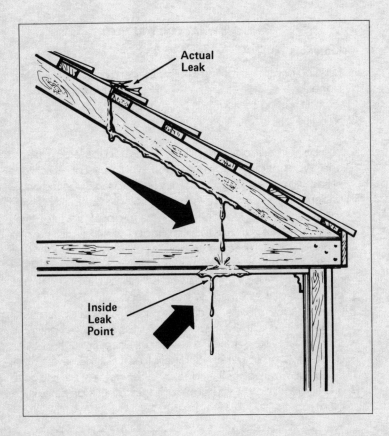

from one direction and with enough force to blow rain in under a broken shingle or through some crack. You frequently have to be in the attic when it is raining in order to track down the spot, but the leak may even be in a place where you cannot spot it from inside the attic; then you have to look outside (NOT while the roof is wet). Look for such things as missing shingles, split shingles, loose nails, or bad flashing. Once you find the leak, mark it well so that you know where to go to work when the roof is dry.

Assuming that you have located the leak, you are ready to make some actual repairs. The following instructions are for a wood shingle roof.

HERE IS WHAT YOU WILL NEED

Materials	Tools
☐ Flashing or asphalt roofing paper	☐ Garden spade
☐ Asphalt roofing cement	☐ Hacksaw blade
☐ Shingles	☐ Propane torch

1. You can either replace a split shingle or stop the leak in the old one. If you decide not to replace the shingle, try slipping a piece of flashing under the split or inserting some asphalt roofing paper under it. First, pry up the overlapping shingle with a flat garden spade, using your foot on the handle to apply pressure. If you cannot get the patch as far back under the shingle as you think it should go, use a hacksaw blade to cut away any nails that are in the way. Then apply asphalt roofing cement to anchor the patch. If you need to drive new nails that leave exposed heads, put a dab of the cement over each head.

2. Replace any missing shingles as soon as you notice their absence. Pry up the overlapping shingles, saw away any nails that prevent your getting the new shingle in far enough, and use a combination of cement and nails to anchor the new shingle.

3. If the problem involves the ridge shingles, your best bet is to go to a lumberyard and buy a bundle of ridges rather than try to piece them together.

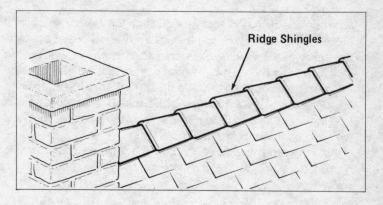

Ridge Shingles

For repairs on composition roof shingles, follow these instructions.

1. Asphalt shingles with curled corners can be tamed easily by putting a dab of asphalt roofing cement about the size of a quarter under each and pressing the corner down.
2. You can patch many holes or rips with roofing cement. Just lift up the shingle, dab the cement under the hole, and press the shingle back down.
3. If you must replace a shingle, you can usually get to the nails holding the faulty shingle by raising the overlapping shingle. Raise it gently so as not to crack the shingle. Then loosen and remove the nails, and slip the bad section out. Put the new one in its place and renail using only two nails. Dab cement on the nail heads and on the overlapping shingle to anchor it down. You will find that warm composition shingles are much more pliable and, therefore, easier to work with. If you cannot do your roof repair work on a hot day, try running the flame from a propane torch across your shingles if they seem too brittle.

You can patch most flashing problems with asphalt roofing cement. The problem here is in locating the trouble. A gap in a flashing joint is easy to spot and easy to patch, but detecting a nearly invisible pinhole is something else again. When you see any spots that might possibly be such pinholes, cover them with cement. In addition, dab a little cement on any exposed nails in the flashing.

Care of Gutters and Downspouts   8

GUTTERS AND DOWNSPOUTS do require a little attention. Most importantly, they need to be kept clean. If the water cannot run along the gutters and pass through the downspouts, it will go over the sides and onto the ground creating water problems under your home as well as a host of other problems. Gutters should always be cleaned after all the leaves have fallen in the autumn, and they may need to be checked at other times as well—depending on the type of trees you have around.

HERE IS WHAT YOU WILL NEED

Materials	Tools
☐ Paint thinner	☐ Ladder
☐ Window screen material	☐ Plastic scoop, or whisk
☐ Asphalt roofing cement	broom
☐ Galvanized roofing nails	☐ Work gloves
☐ Rivets or waterproof duct	☐ Garden hose
tape	☐ Plumber's snake
	☐ Wire brush
	☐ Hammer
	☐ Pop rivet tool
	☐ Drill

1. Use a ladder that is tall enough to reach the gutters, and be sure to play it safe; move the ladder often so that you never have to reach far to either side.

2. Remove all the debris from the gutter. Use a plastic scoop or a

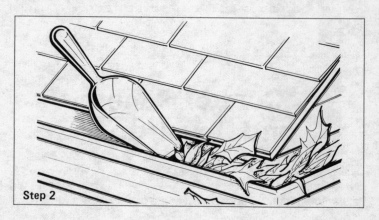

Step 2

whisk broom to rake the leaves out of the gutter. If you clean the gutters with your hands, be sure to wear work gloves.

3. Flush out the gutters with a garden hose.

4. Flush out the downspouts with the hose. If you discover that they are stopped up, use a plumber's snake to break through the clog. Then flush with the hose.

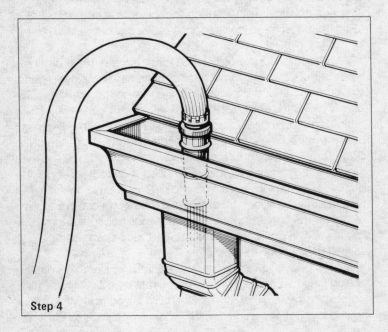

Step 4

While you are cleaning, look for rust spots, holes, loose supports, and sags in the gutters and downspouts. Check the runoff to be sure the gutters are still pitched properly, and be sure the strainers are in place and unclogged.

Gutters with holes can be patched. For an easy way to patch them, follow these step-by-step instructions.

1. Remove all rust and any other loose metal by cleaning the area with a wire brush. Cover the bad spot with paint thinner.

2. Cut a patch from wire window screen material. The patch must cover the hole and extend about ½ inch beyond it.

3. Coat the area around the hole with asphalt roofing cement.

4. Put the patch down over the cement and press it in place.

5. Brush the cement over the screen.

6. When the first coat sets up, cover it again with cement. You can patch tiny holes without using the screen; the cement will fill in by itself. You may have to apply several coats, however.

A gutter that sags usually has a loose hanger. There are three types of gutter hangers in use today. One type employs a gutter spike driven through a sleeve and into the roof board. If the spike comes loose, you can drive it back in with a hammer. Another type features a strap that is nailed to the roof under a shingle. Be sure to use galvanized roofing nails to resecure a loose strap, then put a dab of roofing cement over the heads and old nail holes. The third type of gutter hanger is a bracket nailed to the fascia under the gutter. Since you may not be able to get to the loose nails with this type of gutter hanger, add an auxiliary support of another type to eliminate the sag. Sometimes a gutter sags because it lacks sufficient support points. There should be support points about every 36 inches along the run of gutter.

If an elbow or a section of downspout keeps coming off, the easiest way to attach it permanently is with a pop rivet tool. This is an inexpensive tool that installs rivets from the outside without your having to reach the inside surface. To install pop rivets, follow these steps.

1. Place the two sections together.

2. Using a drill bit of the size specified to accommodate the size rivet you have, drill through both pieces. Make two such holes, one on either side or one at the front and one at the back of the downspout.

3. Insert the rivet into the hole in the tool, and then place the tip into the holes you drilled.

4. Squeeze the handles of the tool together until the rivet shaft pops off. The rivet will then be permanently in place.

If you do not have a pop rivet tool and do not wish to buy one, you can use waterproof duct tape to hold the sections together. Although the tape holds well, you may feel that taped sections look less neat or attractive than riveted sections.

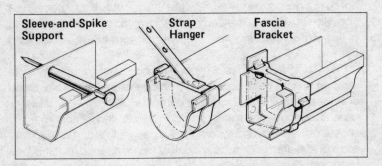

Sleeve-and-Spike Support

Strap Hanger

Fascia Bracket

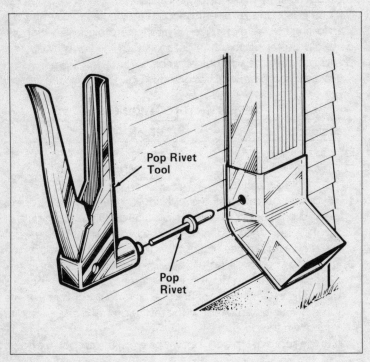

Pop Rivet Tool

Pop Rivet

9 Caulking

CAULKING IS important for three reasons. First, most uncaulked areas look bad. Second, uncaulked cracks can let cold air in and hot air out during the winter, and just the opposite if your house is air conditioned during the summer. And third, a lack of caulking allows water, dirt, and insects to attack your house's paint and framing.

There are five basic types of caulking compounds. Oil base is the least expensive, but it does not last as long as others. Moreover, you cannot paint oil base caulking compounds for 24 hours. A latex base is much longer lasting and can be painted almost immediately. It adheres to most surfaces, weathers well, and cleans up with soap and water. Butyl rubber caulk is also long lived, but it is best used on masonry-to-metal joints. It requires a solvent for clean up. Silicone caulks are excellent because they cure quickly and are long lasting but are expensive. Polyvinyl acetate caulks, which are generally better indoors than outdoors, lack the flexibility of other caulks because they dry hard and brittle.

Here are some general tips on caulking.

HERE IS WHAT YOU WILL NEED

Materials	Tools
☐ Caulk	☐ Knife
☐ Cleaning solvent	☐ Caulk gun

1. Always clean away all the old caulking. It can be scraped, peeled, or gouged, and then pulled away. Once you get rid of all of it, clean the area to be caulked with a solvent. You want the area to be as free of dirt, oil, wax, and dust as possible.

2. Try to do your caulking work in warm weather. If that is not possible, warm the caulking tube itself before you apply its contents. In extremely hot weather, the caulking can get too runny; try placing the tube in the refrigerator for a brief period to slow down the caulk.

3. Cut the spout at a place that will give you the proper size bead

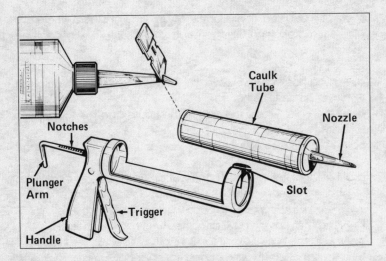

for the job. The bead should overlap onto both surfaces. Cut your spout at an angle.

4. Load the caulking tube into the gun.

5. Hold the gun at a 45-degree angle in the direction of your movement.

6. When you have to stop, twist the L-shaped plunger rod until it disengages in order to stop the caulk from oozing out.

Where should you caulk? As a rule of thumb, any place that has two different parts that come together with a crack in between

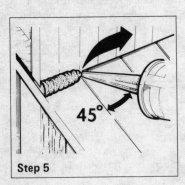

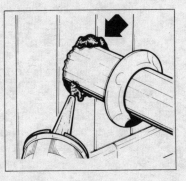

Step 5

should be caulked. Think particularly in terms of places where two different materials come together. Here is a sample list of caulking spots:

a. Around doors and windows where the frame and the side of the house come together.

b. At the point where the side of the house and the foundation meet.

c. In the joint where steps or porches and the main body of the house meet.

d. Where the chimney meets the roof, around the flashing, and the gap in the seam between flashing and shingles.

e. Where plumbing goes through walls to enter the house.

f. Along the seam formed at corners where siding meets.

g. Around the exhaust vent for the clothes dryer.

h. In the spaces between air conditioner window units and window frames.

10 Broken Windows

REPLACING a broken window is a simple job, even if you want to cut the replacement glass to size yourself. Since any hardware store or lumberyard that sells you the glass will cut it to size, however, you can fix the broken pane without ever concerning yourself with the techniques of glass cutting. Here, then, are the basic procedures for pane replacement.

HERE IS WHAT YOU WILL NEED

Materials	Tools	
☐ Linseed oil	☐ Work gloves	☐ Safety goggles
☐ Glazier's compound	☐ Hammer	☐ Wire brush
☐ Replacement pane	☐ Chisel	☐ Paintbrush
☐ Paint	☐ Propane torch	☐ Putty knife

1. Remove all the old glass. Wear work gloves and be careful as you wiggle the pieces of glass back and forth until you free them. If there are pieces that are too firmly imbedded in the putty to come loose with wiggling, take a hammer and knock them out. Wear safety goggles to prevent any injury to your eyes.

2. When the glass is all out, scrape away all the old putty from the frame. You can soften dried putty with heat from a propane torch, or—if you do not have a torch—you can brush the puttied areas with linseed oil and let it soak in. The linseed oil should soften the putty sufficiently to allow you to scrape it away. As you remove the old putty, be on the lookout for little metal tabs (in a wooden frame) or spring clips (in a metal frame) and save them.

3. Use a wire brush to remove the last traces of putty, and coat the area with linseed oil. Just brush it on.

4. Measure the frame across both directions, and subtract $\frac{1}{16}$ inch from each measurement to compensate for the fact that most frames are not perfect rectangles and for the expansion and contraction of the glass that will occur later on. In fact, if there is a wide lip on the frame, subtract as much as $\frac{1}{8}$ inch from both the vertical and horizontal measurements.

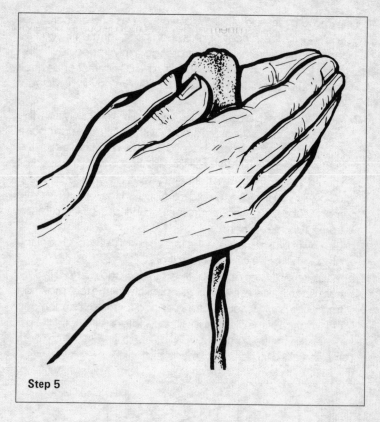

Step 5

5. Roll either glazier's compound or glazing putty (the compound is preferable) between your hands to form a string about as big around as a pencil. Press this string against the outside of the frame where the glass is to fit.

6. When the putty completely covers the lip of the frame, press the glass in place against the putty. Press firmly, and pay no attention to the fact that some of the putty is pushed out around the frame.

7. With the pane pressed firmly in position, insert the glazier's points or spring clips to hold the glass in place. The clips snap in holes, while the points must be pushed into the wood. Use your putty knife to push them in; they need not be pushed in very far. The points should go in about every six to eight inches around the frame.

8. Now you are ready to finish the job by putting putty around the outside of the glass. The object here is to make your new bed of putty look like the others on windows around it. The best way to go about it is to place blobs of putty all around the glass against the frame, and then use your putty knife to smooth them out. If the putty knife seems to stick to the putty and pull it away from the glass and frame, dip the knife in linseed oil (or water) to stop it from doing so.

9. Remove the excess putty from both inside and outside the frame, and put the putty back in the can.

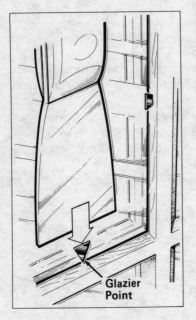

Glazier Point

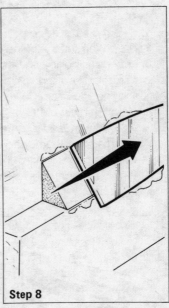

Step 8

10. Allow the putty to cure for three days, and then paint it. Paint all the way from the frame up to the glass, letting a little paint get over on the glass to seal the putty completely.

11 How to Cut Glass

ANY HARDWARE store that sells glass will cut it to your exact specifications, but if you do a great deal of glazing or if you do your own picture framing, you can save money by doing the cutting yourself. With a little practice, the right tools, and proper instructions, you can be cutting glass to size in no time. Just follow these steps.

HERE IS WHAT YOU WILL NEED

Materials	Tools
☐ Machine oil or kerosene	☐ Glass cutter
☐ Finishing nails	☐ Straightedge
☐ Fine wet-dry sandpaper	

1. Select a flat surface on which your piece of glass will fit.
2. Clean the surface of the glass.
3. Lubricate the tiny wheel on the glass cutter with machine oil or kerosene. You should also brush a film of the lubricant along the line you intend to cut.
4. Hold the glass cutter between your index and middle fingers, with your index finger resting against the flat area on the handle. Your thumb should be on the handle's bottom side. Grip the cutter firmly but not too tightly.
5. Place a straightedge along the line to be cut, and hold it firmly in place.

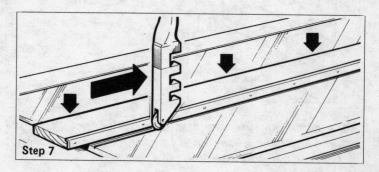

Step 7

6. Position the cutter so that it is almost at a right angle to the glass.

7. Start your cut about ⅛ inch (or less) from the edge farthest from you. The stroke must be an even flowing motion toward you that continues until the cutter goes off the near edge. The idea is not to cut through the glass, but merely to score it. Experiment with scrap pieces of glass to discover how much pressure you must apply to attain an even scoring. Never let up on the cutter and never go back over the line.

8. As soon as you score the glass, make the break. Glass heals, and if you wait too long it will not snap along the line. The idea in snapping is to provide a raised area under the scored line. Some people position the glass so that the cut is along the edge of the table, and then they snap the glass along the table edge. Others slip a pencil under the glass and center it on the line, while still others place finishing nails at each end of the scored line.

9. To make the snap, press down on the glass firmly on both sides of the line.

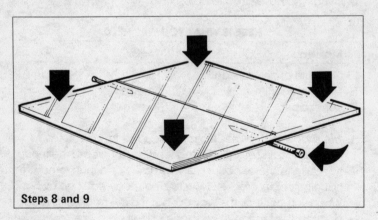

Steps 8 and 9

10. Smooth the newly cut edge with fine wet-dry sandpaper.

Keep the wheel of the glass cutter well lubricated between uses, and protect the wheel from anything that might nick or dull it.

12 Window Shades

ANY SHADE THAT refuses to go up and down and stay up or down the way you want it is a pain in the neck. Some shades are so wound up that they could almost lift you off the ground, while others are so slack that they fail to go up at all. In most cases, the remedy is just a matter of adjustment; but in order to know how to adjust a shade properly, you should understand how one works.

Look at the deceptively simple-looking wooden roller. One end of the roller is hollow, with a concealed coil spring in it. There is a pin at either end of the roller; the one at the spring end is flat and rotates, winding or unwinding the spring. When you stop pulling, a little lever—called a pawl—falls in place against a ratchet at the spring end of the roller. The pawl prevents the spring from winding the shade back up. When you wish to raise the shade, you tug down slightly on the shade, moving the pawl away from the ratchet and allowing the spring to carry the shade back up. Now that you know how a shade works, you should have no problem in figuring out what you have to do to adjust it.

HERE IS WHAT YOU WILL NEED

Materials	Tools
☐ Graphite or dry lubricant	☐ Pliers
☐ Cardboard shim	☐ Screwdriver
☐ Sandpaper	☐ Hammer

1. The shade that refuses to go back up as far as you would like obviously lacks sufficient spring tension. To increase the tension, first pull the shade about halfway down, and then remove the flat pin from its bracket. Now roll the shade back up by hand. When you get it all the way up, put the pin back in its bracket and test the tension. If the shade still will not go up far enough, repeat this procedure until the spring tension is just right.
2. If the shade wants to pull you up with it, you must decrease the spring tension. To do so, take the flat pin out of its bracket while the shade is up and unroll it by hand about halfway; then return

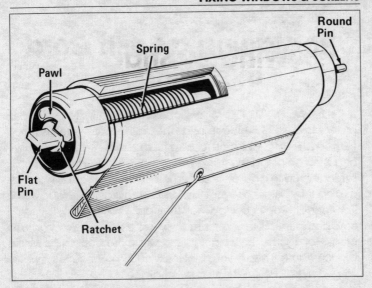

the pin to its bracket and see whether you have tamed your shade's spring tension sufficiently.

3. If the shade fails to stay down, you know that for some reason the pawls are not catching. Remove the metal cap from the flat-pin end of the roller; then clean and lubricate the pawl and ratchet mechanism. You can use either graphite or a dry lubricant.

4. A shade that wobbles when it goes up or down usually has a bent pin. Apply gentle pressure with a pair of pliers to straighten the pin.

5. When a shade falls out of its brackets, you must move the brackets closer together. If the brackets are mounted inside the window casing, you must add a shim behind the brackets. Usually, a cardboard shim will do. If the brackets are mounted outside the window casing, you can either reposition them or bend them slightly toward each other.

6. A shade that rubs is the victim of brackets that are too close together. You can move outside brackets farther apart, but you must resort to other techniques for those mounted inside the window casing. First, try to tap the brackets lightly with a hammer. If that does not move them enough, take the metal cap and fixed round pin off the roller, and sand down the wood a bit.

13 Replacing a Sash Cord in a Window

MOST WOOD WINDOWS are operated by a system of ropes, pulleys, and weights hidden inside the wall. The ropes are attached to the *sash*—a fancy name for a frame that moves up and down—and then go along the tracks in which the window moves, finally extending up to a pulley and then is tied to the weight, which acts as a counterbalance so that the window stays at the level to which you raise it. Ropes being what they are, though, they become frayed and then break after many years of service. When a rope breaks, of course, the weight falls down to the bottom inside the window frame. It also means that the window no longer stays where you want it to. Here is the step-by-step cure.

HERE IS WHAT YOU WILL NEED

Materials	Tools
☐ Replacement cord or sash chain	☐ Razor blade
	☐ Putty knife or flat bar
	☐ Hammer
	☐ Screwdriver

1. Remove the stop molding from the side where the cord is broken, but do it carefully or the molding might break. If there is a paint seal along the molding strip, cut it with a sharp razor blade. Then use a wide putty knife blade or a flat bar to pry the stop molding out.
2. With the stop strip out of the way, angle the sash out of the frame to expose the pocket in which the rope is knotted.
3. Untie the knot and remove the rope from the sash frame.
4. Ease the sash out of its track on the other side, and untie the rope there. Knot this rope to prevent it from disappearing inside the wall.
5. Set the entire sash out of the way.
6. Look for the access plate. You should be able to locate it in the lower part of the track, but it may have been painted over

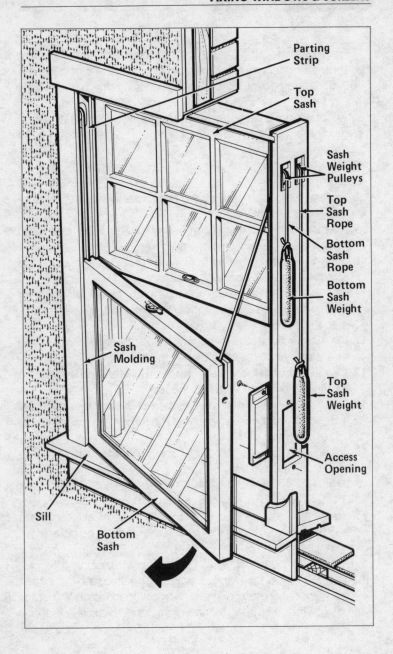

Parting Strip

Top Sash

Sash Weight Pulleys

Top Sash Rope

Bottom Sash Rope

Bottom Sash Weight

Top Sash Weight

Access Opening

Sash Molding

Sill

Bottom Sash

several times. If it is hidden by the paint, tap the track with a hammer until you reveal the outline. Then cut along the line with a sharp razor blade. Once you locate the access plate, find the screws holding it in place and remove them. (Some older windows do not have access plates; if that is what you find, you must pry the entire frame out to get at the weight inside.)

7. With the access plate removed, you will see the weight. Lift it out.

8. Untie the old cord and use the two broken pieces to measure the replacement cord.

9. Weight the new cord with something small enough to be fed in over the pulley, and feed the cord in.

10. When the cord reaches the access plate opening, pull the cord through the opening.

11. Remove the small weight you had to put on earlier, and knot the cord to the regular window weight. Put the weight back into the access hole.

12. Tie the cord opposite the one you have been working with to the sash, and reinsert the sash in the track.

13. Tie the new cord to the sash, and then hold the sash against the parting strip as you raise it to the top.

14. Inspect the weight at the access hole. It should be about three inches above the sill as you hold the sash at the top. If it is not, adjust the rope at the sash.

15. When you get the weight properly adjusted, replace the access plate and the stop strip.

If the broken cord is in the upper sash of a double hung window, you follow the same procedure except that you must remove the parting strip after removing the lower sash in order to be able to get at the upper sash.

That is all there is to it. As long as you are replacing the cord, though, you should think about replacing it with a sash chain that will not wear out or break or stretch as rope does. The chain comes with a hook that you fasten to the weight and with a spring that you attach to the sash.

Holes in Screens

14

SCREENS ARE GREAT when they let in air and light and keep out the bugs, but they always seem to develop holes. Patching is the way to cure most small holes in screens.

HERE IS WHAT YOU WILL NEED

Materials	Tools
☐ Clear nail polish or shellac	☐ Ice pick (or any pointed
☐ Strand of wire or strong	tool)
nylon thread	☐ Small brush
☐ Needle	☐ Scissors
☐ Screening material	☐ Electric iron
☐ Fiberglass patch	
☐ Aluminum foil	

Step 1

1. For a tiny hole, use an ice pick (or any pointed object) to move as many strands as possible back toward the hole. If none of the wire strands are torn, you can close the hole back up and make the screen as good as new.

2. Unfortunately, there generally are a few torn strands. If that is the case, you can close up the hole by painting over it with either clear nail polish or shellac. Brush on a coat and let it dry; then keep applying more coats until the hole is sealed over.

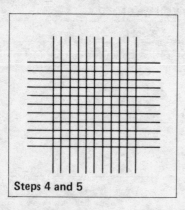

Steps 4 and 5

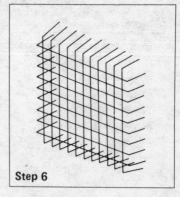

Step 6

3. If the hole is a long rip, you may need to stitch it back together. Once again, close the gap with your sharp pointed tool, and then use a strand of wire or a strong nylon thread to bind up the wound. A needle will make the sewing go quicker, and a few coats of clear polish or shellac will prevent the stitching from unraveling.
4. For a bigger hole, cut a square—at least two inches bigger than the hole all the way around—from a separate piece of screening.
5. Pick away a few strands of wire on all four sides to leave about ½ inch of unwoven strands sticking out.
6. Fold the unwoven edges forward, and insert these wires into the screen over the hole.
7. Fold the unwoven strands toward the center of the patch on the opposite side, and stitch around the patch with a needle and nylon thread. Once again, a few coats of nail polish or shellac will seal the patch and stitching in place.
8. Repair fiberglass screening by laying a patch of the material over the hole and running a hot iron around the edges. Be sure to place a scrap of foil over the screen itself to prevent the iron from touching it. The heat melts and fuses the patch in place.

Screen Replacement

15

WHEN YOU SPOT a hole in your screen door or window screen that is too large to patch, you should start thinking about replacing the entire screen. In most cases you can buy screen cut to the proper width for standard doors or windows, and the actual installation of the new screen is not difficult—provided, of course, that the frame is still in good shape. The secret to any good rescreening job is knowing how to get the screen taut.

First, consider replacing a screen in a wooden frame.

HERE IS WHAT YOU WILL NEED

Materials	Tools
☐ Replacement screening	☐ Putty knife
☐ Staples	☐ Pliers
	☐ C-clamps or metal weight
	☐ 2x4s
	☐ Worktable or sawhorse
	☐ Staple gun
	☐ Scissors or wire cutters
	☐ Splining tool

1. Remove the molding from around the edges of the screen, but be sure to pry carefully so as not to damage the molding. Leave the brads in the molding.

2. Remove the old screen, which is either tacked or stapled in place. Be sure to remove all the old tacks or staples.

3. Now you need to bow or arch the frame. Use either the weighted method or the clamp method.

4. With the frame arched, use a staple gun to attach the screen at each end; stapling is much quicker than tacking. Staple every two or three inches along the top and bottom of the frame.

5. When the screen is fastened securely to the frame, release the

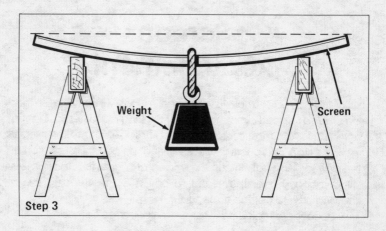

Weight

Screen

Step 3

weights or clamps. The screen should be very taut as the frame straightens out.

6. Trim off any excess screening, reinstall the molding, and the job is done.

With aluminum frames, you must examine the spline to see that it is still in good shape. The spline is a sort of rubber rope that holds the screening in the track all around the frame.

1. Remove the old screen and spline.
2. Position the new screen (about as wide as the entire frame) over the frame, aligning one end and one side of the screen with the corresponding edges of the frame.
3. For best results, you should have a splining wheel to insert the new screen in the frame. Use the end with the convex roller to push the screening down into the groove, working on the end and side you just aligned with the frame. Then do the remaining two sides. The screen should be quite taut.
4. Now you are ready to reinstall the spline. Use the other end of the tool—the concave wheel—to work the spline into the track all the way around the frame.
5. Trim off any excess screening, and your aluminum screen is as good as new.

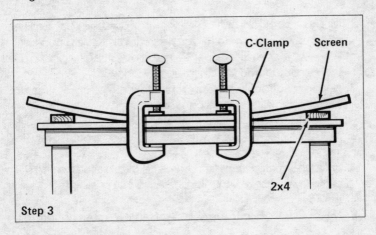

Step 3

16 Weather-Stripping Windows

IF YOUR WINDOWS are letting cold air in during the winter and cold air out during the summer, you are losing a great deal of money to the utility companies. It will pay you to check your windows' weather stripping for airtightness. If you can reach the windows from the outside, direct the airflow from a hand-held dryer all around the frame as someone inside follows your movements and marks the bad spots.

If your windows have no weather stripping at all, you can install it without much trouble. You can use the spring-metal type or the pressure-sensitive adhesive backed type or the vinyl-tubular type. All are easy to install. The following instructions are for the vinyl-tubular type of weather stripping.

HERE IS WHAT YOU WILL NEED

Materials	Tools
☐ Vinyl-tubular weather stripping	☐ Hand-held hair dryer
☐ Brads	☐ Ladder
	☐ Hammer

1. Measure all cracks that could allow the passage of air to determine how much material you need. If you have a number of windows, it is often less expensive to buy weather stripping in bulk than to buy individual rolls for each window.
2. Since you attach vinyl-tubular weather stripping from the outside of each window, you can save yourself several trips up and down the ladder by cutting the strips before you start climbing.
3. Nail the strips in place with brads placed about every two inches.
4. Install the vertical strips first, attaching them to the parting strips of the lower sash. The tubular portion should press lightly against the sash.
5. Next, attach a strip to the outside of the lower sash bottom rail in

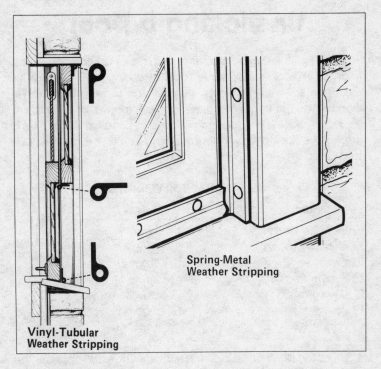

Spring-Metal
Weather Stripping

Vinyl-Tubular
Weather Stripping

such a way that the tubular portion will rest snugly against the outside sill when the window is down.

6. Attach the strip for the upper sash bottom rail with the tubular part facing in toward the lower sash and positioned so that it will press lightly against the lower sash when it is down.

7. If the upper sash is movable, you must attach strips to the blind stop and a strip across the top of the yoke.

Vinyl-tubular weather stripping is very easy to install if the windows are easily accessible from the outside. It is also very effective when installed properly, and it will last a long time. The big disadvantage to such weather stripping is the fact that it cannot be painted; paint often makes vinyl-tubular weather stripping stiff and reduces its effectiveness. In addition, the vinyl-tubular type is probably the least attractive kind of weather stripping.

17 Unsticking a Door

FEW THINGS ARE more annoying than a sticking door. When you finally do get it open, you cannot get it closed again. Unfortunately, most homeowners grab a plane and start shaving away some wood. Although frequently there is no alternative, planing down your door should be a measure of last resort. The first thing to do is inspect the door to see what is causing it to stick. Here are the steps to follow.

HERE IS WHAT YOU WILL NEED

Materials	Tools
☐ Wooden toothpicks	☐ Plane
☐ Shim (shirtboard)	☐ Hammer
☐ Chalk	☐ C-clamp
☐ Penetrating oil	☐ Carpenter's square
☐ Large wooden box	☐ Screwdriver
☐ Paint	☐ Large nail
☐ Padded 2x4	

1. Close the door, if possible, and examine the edge opposite the sticking place. If you see a large gap there, the problem may well be in the hinges.
2. If there are no gaps—or very few—anywhere around the door, then the wood probably is swollen with moisture.
3. Open the door and place a carpenter's square against the frame to see whether it is out of line. If that is what you find, then the house has probably settled and forced the frame out of shape.

If your diagnosis is a hinge problem, here are the steps you should follow.

1. Check all the screws in the hinges to see that they are tight. If any continue to turn, it means that the screw holes have become enlarged. Insert pieces of toothpick into the hole, reinsert the

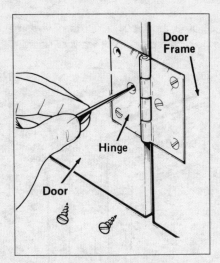

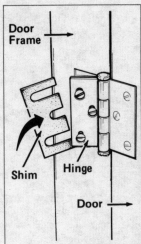

screw, and you should find that the screw bites securely.

2. If the hinges are not loose, they may need to be shimmed up or recessed to relieve the sticking problem. Look at the door to see where it is rubbing. A door that sticks toward the top of the latch side and down at the bottom against the floor is a door that is tilted out at the top. Bring the bottom hinge out a bit, and you may solve the problem. Try cutting a piece of shirtboard to fit between the bottom hinge and the doorjamb; then slot the cardboard so that you only have to loosen the screws to insert the shim. Retighten and see if the shim cures the problem. If it helps but does not eliminate the problem, add another thickness of shim. Naturally, if the door sticks toward the bottom of the latch side, you should shim out the top hinge. If the door sticks along the latch side and there is no gap along the hinge side, you can sometimes cut a deeper mortice in the jamb to set the hinge deeper and move the door away from the frame on the latch side. Similarly, if the door sticks at the top and there is more than ¼-inch space at the bottom, you could consider moving the hinges down a bit.

When you determine that the door is swollen with excess moisture and is just too big for the frame, then you have to remove some of the wood. Here is how to go about planing down your door.

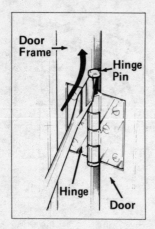 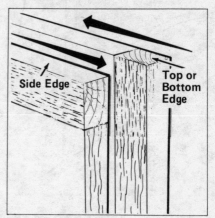

1. Mark the sticking places with a piece of chalk.

2. If the door binds along the top, you can plane without first removing the door from its hinges. Just make sure that when planing the top (or bottom) you cut from the edge toward the center; otherwise, the plane could catch the side rail and rip off a piece of the door.

3. If the door sticks along the side, remove the door by tapping out the hinge pins. Always remove the bottom pin first. Place the tip of a screwdriver under the pin, and tap the screwdriver handle with a hammer. If the pin refuses to budge, insert a nail into the bottom of the hinge and tap upward. Penetrating oil can also help loosen stubborn pins.

4. Once the pins are out the door is free, so hold it securely.

5. Anchor the door to a large wooden box with a C-clamp to help keep the door upright during planing.

6. When planing the side, always cut toward the edges. Keep in mind that the latch side is slightly beveled to prevent the edge from striking the frame when you close the door. Therefore, try to plane the hinge side instead; but if you must plane the latch side, make sure your planing retains this bevel.

7. After you plane all the chalked spots, put the door back on the hinges and give it a trial run.

8. Once you get the door to open and close easily, paint the newly planed areas and any other bare wood to prevent future moisture problems.

If the door frame is out of line from the house having settled, there is little you can do. Try placing a padded 2x4 against the frame, and then hitting the padded board several times with a hammer. Sometimes you can reset the frame just enough to allow the door to pass without sticking. If that does not work, try moving the hinges or planing off enough wood to make the door fit the misaligned frame.

Making Your Home More Secure   18

RESIDENTIAL burglaries occur all too frequently. While there is no way to make your home absolutely burglarproof, you can make it somewhat less vulnerable. Here are some steps you can take to deter a burglar from your home.

HERE IS WHAT YOU WILL NEED

Materials	Tools
☐ Deadbolt locks	☐ Screwdriver
☐ Wide-angle viewer	☐ Hammer
☐ Sheet-metal screws	
☐ Rods or pipes	
☐ Extra window locks	

1. Install a deadbolt lock on every outside door. Many doorknobs have the convenient spring-catch locks, but these locks are also convenient for the burglar. A spring-catch lock can be opened with nothing more than a plastic credit card. Your lock dealer will be happy to show you how to install deadbolts, and the job itself is usually a snap.

2. Install a wide-angle viewer on each outside door to permit members of your family to see who is calling without opening the door.
3. Prepare a rod or pipe to fit in the bottom track of every sliding glass door. In addition, if the sliding door is of the type that can be lifted out of its track for repair, install three sheet-metal screws in the track above the door at its closed position. If you should ever need to lift the door out, slide it open and remove the screws.
4. Provide an auxiliary lock or pin on windows so that no one can merely break the glass, reach in, and open the window.
5. Check to see if shrubbery hides doors and windows from view. Such shrubs might allow an intruder to break in without being seen.
6. When you leave—even for just a few moments—lock up.
7. Always keep your garage locked.
8. Avoid leaving tools and ladders outside where a burglar could use them to his advantage.
9. When you are outside doing yard work, keep all doors locked.
10. Keep all gates to your yard locked.
11. Provide good lighting all around your home, and keep it on all night long. Burglars seldom like to be seen on the job.
12. Check the Crime Prevention Department of your local police department and ask about a property identification program. This program enables you to borrow an electric engraver to mark your valuables. You should, of course, always maintain a record of the serial numbers from your appliances, guns, TV sets, VCRs, and stereos.

How to Install a New Lock 19

MANY PEOPLE are upgrading the locks around their homes. One of the best moves you can make is to put a deadbolt cylinder lock above the present knob. This additional lock may increase the amount of time it takes you to get into your house, but it provides important extra protection. Installation is not complicated. Here is how you can put in a new lock in very little time.

HERE IS WHAT YOU WILL NEED

Materials	Tools
☐ New lock	☐ Drill
☐ Large escutcheon plate	☐ Expansion bit
	☐ Wood chisel
	☐ Screwdriver

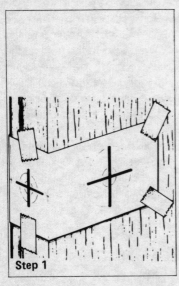

Step 1

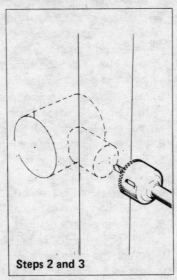

Steps 2 and 3

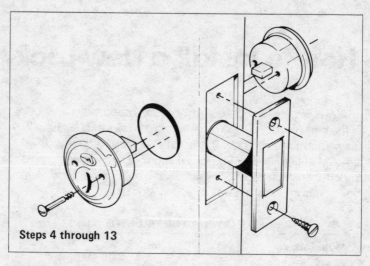

Steps 4 through 13

1. The new lock will come with a paper template that fits around the door's edge to permit you to mark the two holes. One hole goes through the side of the door for the cylinder, while the other goes into the edge of the door for the bolt.

2. Use a hand brace and an expansion bit to drill a hole of the size specified for your lock, but be careful not to damage the veneer on the sides of the door. When you see the point of the drill coming through, stop and go around to the other side to finish the hole. You avoid splintering the door that way.

3. Drill a hole of the appropriate size for the bolt into the edge of the door. Be sure to drill at a right angle to the door, and keep drilling until you reach the cylinder hole.

4. Insert the bolt into its hole, and mark the area for the plate.

5. Remove the bolt, and mortice out for the plate to make it fit flush. Use a wood chisel to cut the mortice.

6. Insert the plate in the mortice, and drill pilot holes for the screws.

7. Install the screws to secure the bolt in place.

8. Insert the outside cylinder so that the stems or the connecting bar fit into the bolt assembly.

9. Attach the interior cylinder and secure it with screws.

10. Locate the proper spot for the strike plate on the jamb.

11. Drill the required size hole.

12. Use the plate as a pattern, mark the jamb for morticing, and cut the mortice.

13. Install the plate with screws so that it fits flush with the jamb.

If you just want to replace an existing lock with a better one, look for a new lock that will fit in the existing holes. Sometimes you will not be able to cover the old holes with the new lock, but you can generally cover them with a large decorative escutcheon plate. If need be, you can usually enlarge mortices and holes to accommodate the new lock.

Weather-Stripping a Door 20

IF YOU CAN feel little gusts of cold air coming in around the door during the winter, or if you have a door that hums a note or two when the wind blows, you better check your weather stripping. All of your outside doors should be airtight, and the same holds true for inner doors to unheated basements, garages, and attics. Proper weather stripping will save you money during heating and air conditioning seasons.

There is really only one way to check a door's weather stripping. You must direct a strong wind against it to see if air comes through. The best way is to use a hand-held hair dryer outside and have a helper inside. As you move the stream of air along the door, have your helper hold his hand against the crack between the door and the frame and mark with chalk any places where he feels air coming through. Take your time and make a thorough check. If you have just a few minor air leaks, you may be able to fix your present weather stripping. Most doors have a springy metal strip that fits against the door jamb all the way around except at the bottom. See if you can bend the metal flange out a little more to stop any leaks.

If the existing weather stripping is not doing its job, you can add additional protection outside the jamb. The easiest type to install is the foam-rubber strip that has a pressure sensitive adhesive backing.

HERE IS WHAT YOU WILL NEED

Materials	Tools
☐ Chalk	☐ Hand-held hair dryer
☐ Foam-rubber weather stripping	☐ Scissors
☐ Cleaning solvent	☐ Hammer
☐ Nails	☐ Screwdriver
☐ Replacement threshold	☐ Hacksaw
☐ Metal-strip weather stripping	☐ Tin snips
☐ Brads	

1. Unroll enough of the stripping to go around the top and both sides of the door.
2. Cut the strip into pieces to fit each of these three sections.
3. Open the door and clean the face of the jamb.
4. Let the wood dry.
5. Peel the backing off of the strip and apply the foam rubber to the face of the jamb so that the door closes against it.
6. Recheck the door for leaks.

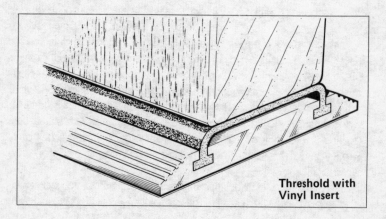

Threshold with Vinyl Insert

If the leak is at the bottom of the door, you may need a new threshold. If the threshold is the problem, you can put a new one in easily.

Aluminum thresholds with vinyl flaps that seal against the door come packed with all the screws and instructions. You can cut the aluminum to size with a hacksaw.

There are also strips of both wood and metal that you attach to the jamb with nails. You fit these strips so that they will be snug against the closed door, and then you nail them in place.

1. Unroll enough of the thin metal weather stripping for the hinge side of the door. Use tin snips to cut to the exact size required.
2. Place the strip against the jamb so that the springy part that flares out faces to the outside and is almost against the stop.
3. Nail the strip in place by driving tiny brads in about every two inches. Tack the strip at top and bottom first to make sure that it goes on straight.
4. For the latch side, attach the folded strip that comes with the roll right next to the striker plate. If there is no such strip with the roll, you can purchase one separately.
5. Cut the strips to fit above and below, and nail them in place.
6. Cut the strip for the top, miter it at each end, and then nail it in place.

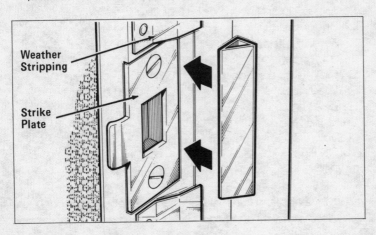

Weather Stripping

Strike Plate

21 Refinishing Hardwood Floors

DESPITE ALL OF the fantastic new easy-to-apply flooring materials, there are few that can beat the beauty of hardwood floors—when they are in good condition, that is. By the same token, a hardwood floor in bad condition can look terrible. If you now have ugly hardwood floors, you can either cover them with carpet or you can restore their beauty.

The best way to remove the old worn-out finish is to sand it off. When you look at an average-size room, though, and think about how long it will take to sand, you may wish to give up and forget about refinishing. Fortunately, you can rent a large drum sander that does the job quickly. When you go to the rental company, have the dealer show you how to operate the unit properly. The same holds true for the other sander you will need for the edges. This tool is a disc sander, commonly called a floor edger.

HERE IS WHAT YOU WILL NEED

Materials	Tools
☐ Tape	☐ Drum sander
☐ Coarse (20 grit) open coat sandpaper	☐ Disc sander
☐ Medium (40 grit) sandpaper	☐ Sanding block
☐ Fine (100 grit) sandpaper	☐ Putty knife
☐ Wood stain	☐ Nailset
☐ Turpentine	☐ Vacuum cleaner
☐ Rags	☐ Paintbrush
☐ Synthetic varnish or other floor finish	☐ Buffer
☐ Wax	

1. Move all of the furniture and plants out of the room, and take down any wall hangings.

2. Tape over all heating and air conditioning ducts.

3. Carefully remove the shoe molding (quarter round).

4. Check the entire floor for nail heads. If you find any, use a nailset to drive them below the surface.

5. When you finish all of the preparatory steps, open all the windows and close the doors to adjoining rooms.

6. For the initial sanding, place coarse (20 grit) open coat sandpaper on the drum sander. Go over the entire floor with the sander, sanding with the grain. Since the sander works in both

Drum Sander

directions, you make one pass pushing and another pulling. You must tilt the unit to raise the drum at the beginning and end of each pass. Lower it back slowly each time to prevent it from digging into the floor. Proceed slowly, never let the machine run away with you or stand in one place while it is running. Go over the edges with the disc sander, using the same grit abrasive. To get right up in the corners, however, you must use a sanding block equipped with the same grit sandpaper.

7. When you finish the first sanding, change to a medium sandpaper, a 40 grit. Repeat the same sanding procedure.

8. Next comes the final sanding. Use a fine or 100 grit sandpaper.

9. Return the rented equipment.

10. Vacuum the room thoroughly to get all of the dust out.

11. The next step is optional; it is a matter of personal taste whether to stain the floor or leave it the natural color. For a pretty good idea of how the natural wood will look without a stain but with a finish, take a rag and rub turpentine over a small section of the floor. What you see is quite close to the way the floor will look with just a finish on it. If you think it is too light, then staining is the answer.

12. After you stain the floor or decide against staining, you must apply the finish. The most popular finishes today are synthetic varnishes—such as polyurethane—but you should consult your paint dealer and let him show you samples of how each finish will look on your floor. Whatever type you decide to apply, be sure to follow the directions on the label. Put down at least two coats of the finish on your floor. Let dry according to directions.

13. Most finishes wear better when given a periodic waxing. Wax the floor and then buff the new finish when it is completely dry.

22 Squeaking Floors

NEARLY ALL floor squeaks are the result of two pieces of wood rubbing against each other. If you know where the loose boards are, there are some simple remedies you can try.

If you have exposed hardwood floors and if the rubbing occurs between boards of this top flooring, an easy way to stop the noise is to sprinkle talcum powder over the area and sweep it back and forth until you get the powder to go down between the cracks. Talc acts as a dry lubricant, and even though the boards will still move, there will be no more squeaks. Liquid floor wax will accomplish the same thing as the talc. There are more permanent ways to stop squeaks—and they are almost as easy. The best way to attack floor squeaks is from underneath.

HERE IS WHAT YOU WILL NEED

Materials	Tools
☐ Talcum powder or liquid floor wax	☐ Hammer
	☐ Screwdriver
☐ Chalk	☐ Drill
☐ Wooden wedges	☐ Nailset
☐ Wood screws	
☐ Finishing nails	
☐ Wood filler	
☐ Padded wood block	

1. Go to the basement or crawl space under the floor, and have someone on the floor above step on the squeaky spot. If you can see any movement in the subfloor, mark the spots with chalk.
2. Drive wedges in between the joists and the subflooring to stop the boards from moving. You can fashion wedges from scrap shingles or other scrap lumber.
3. If the wedges are no help, use wood screws to pull the subflooring and surface flooring together. Make sure, however, that the screws are not so long as to go all the way through the floor and stick up into the room above.
4. If you cannot reach the floor from underneath, drive six penny (2-inch) finishing nails through the cracks of the hardwood flooring at points around the squeaking boards. Drive the nails in at an angle so that each nail goes through both of the two adjoin-

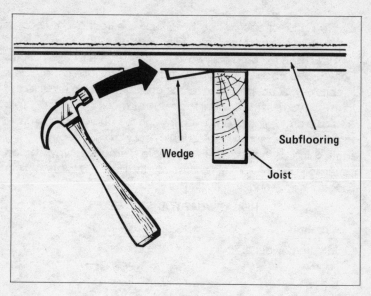

Wedge

Subflooring

Joist

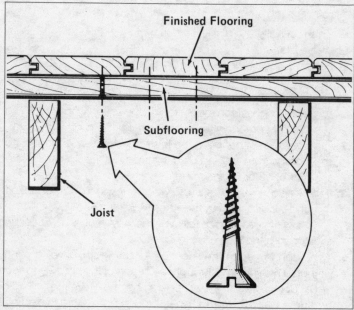

Finished Flooring

Subflooring

Joist

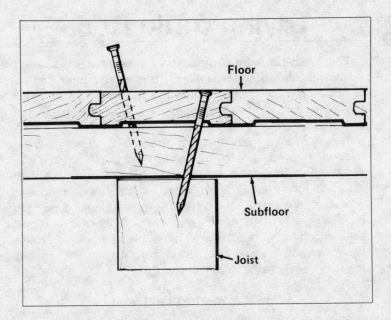

ing boards. Be sure to drill a pilot hole first, before you drive a nail into hardwood. Then, after the nails are in, drive them below the surface with a nailset and hide them with wood filler.

5. You also attack from above if the movement is between the top flooring and the subfloor. Drive ten penny (3-inch) finishing nails through the center of hardwood planks and on into the subfloor below. Again, drive the nails at a slight angle, and then counter-sink and hide them as mentioned above.

6. If the floors are covered with carpet, vinyl, or some other cover-ing—and if there is no way to work from underneath—you may have to tolerate the squeaks or else learn how to dodge the bad spots. Nevertheless, there is one thing you can try: Put padding over the floor, and then pound a block of wood with a hammer to reseat the loose nails. Move the block in an area about two to three feet all around the squeak, tapping sharply with the ham-mer. If the floor still squeaks, then wait until it is time to recover the floors. With the old flooring out of the way, you can drive wood screws in to pull the subflooring tight against the joists.

23 Laying a Tile Floor

IF YOU REALLY want a professional appearance to a do-it-yourself project, put down a resilient tile floor. In a matter of only a few hours, you can change a drab floor into one that will perk up the entire room. You will be amazed at how easily and quickly the work goes.

Floor tiles now come in a wide range of prices and materials. The two most popular types are asphalt tiles and vinyl tiles. The use to which you put the room, the type of subflooring that is already down, and the availability of patterns will have much to do with your selection of tile. Spend some time in choosing your pattern. Purchasing right adhesive is important too. Different materials and different subfloors require different mastics. No matter what type of tiles you choose, however, the procedures for installation are about the same. Here are the steps to follow.

HERE IS WHAT YOU WILL NEED

Materials	Tools
☐ Sandpaper	☐ Putty knife
☐ Chalk	☐ Heavy-duty scissors
☐ Asphalt or vinyl tiles	☐ Rolling pin
☐ Adhesive	☐ Paintbrush or roller or thin-notched flooring trowel

1. The first step—preparation—is the most important one. Pry up the moldings; remove all wax and dirt from the floor surface; search for and sand down any high spots; and make sure there are no nails sticking up. Since resilient tiles are flexible and will conform to whatever is under them, any irregularities in the subfloor will eventually show through. And unless the subflooring is solid, the tiles will loosen.

2. Next, find the exact center of each wall and draw chalk lines from these points across the floor. Where the two lines intersect is the center of the room.

3. Lay a full run of loose (uncemented) tiles from the center of each wall within one quarter of the room. If the last tile in either direction is less than half the width of a full tile, draw a new chalk line beside the actual center line, moving the original line half a tile in either direction. This technique will give you even-sized end tiles at both ends of the room.

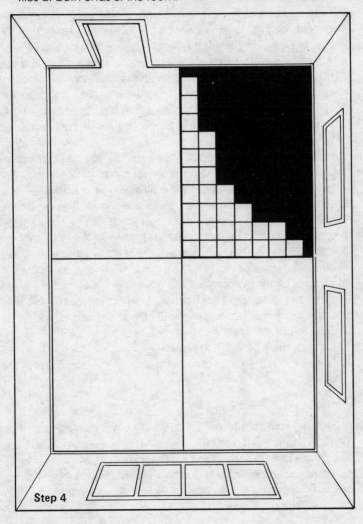

Step 4

4. Now you are ready to start cementing the tiles down. Work on a quarter of the room at a time. Be sure that you check the back of each tile to see that all of the arrows are aimed in the same direction. This keeps the pattern, if any, aligned. If you are using a mixed tile pattern, you should lay it out without mastic before putting the tiles in place. If you have tiles with the adhesive already on the backing, peel off the release paper. Start at the center point, and place the tile down precisely on both lines. It will not slide into place; once down, it is down for good. If you have tiles without mastic, spread the cement over the first quarter only, bringing it right up to the lines. Be sure to use the proper mastic, and follow the directions regarding how long to wait before setting the tiles in place. Usually, you are instructed to wait until the adhesive is tacky.

5. After you get the first center tile in place, lay tiles alternately toward each wall, building a sort of pyramid until the entire quarter is covered except for the tiles along the edges.

6. To cut and fit the border tiles, first place a loose tile (#1) on the last tile in the row. Then butt another loose tile (#2) against the wall, with its sides aligned with those of the #1 tile. Now, make a mark on the #1 tile, along the edge of #2 where the two tiles overlap. If you then cut the #1 tile along the line, you will have an exact fit for the border tile. If you have any irregularities (such as pipes), to fit tiles around, make a paper pattern of the obstacle, trace it onto the tile, and then cut along the line. You should be able to cut most tiles with heavy-duty scissors.

7. Go over the tiles with a rolling pin.

8. Follow the same procedures for the other three quarters of the room.

Here are some tips that will make the job easier. Make sure that the temperature of the room is at least 70 degrees before you start, put all the boxes of tile in this room for at least 24 hours prior to putting them down, and keep the temperature at that level for about a week afterward. Wait at least a week after installation before washing the floor.

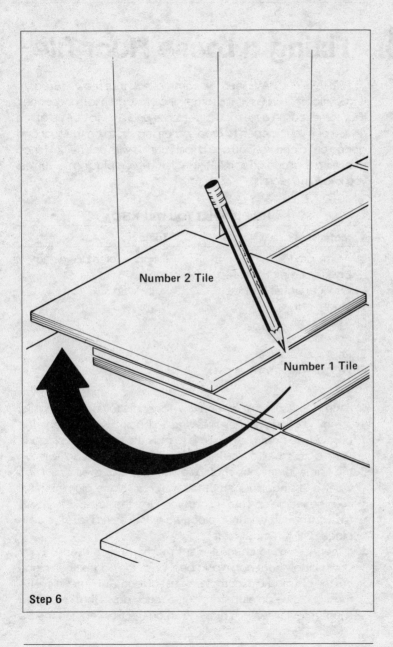

Number 2 Tile

Number 1 Tile

Step 6

24 Fixing a Loose Floor Tile

PERHAPS YOU HAVE seen the commercials that show how easy it is to lay floor tiles yourself. It is something else again to fix loose ones. If for some reason a tile should get loose and start to curl up at the ends—or if you happen to drop something sharp on the floor and gouge out a chunk—you could find yourself with one heck of a job removing that one tile and either regluing it or replacing it . . . unless you know the secrets.

HERE IS WHAT YOU WILL NEED

Materials	Tools
☐ Aluminum foil	☐ Propane torch or electric
☐ Dry ice or metal pot filled	iron
with ice, water, and ice	☐ Putty knife
cream salt	☐ Hammer
☐ Sandpaper	
☐ Floor tile mastic	
☐ Replacement tile	
☐ Weights (i.e., heavy books)	

1. If the tile is loose just around the edges, try to heat the mastic; sometimes you can then press the tile back down for keeps. The best way to heat the mastic is to play the flame of a propane torch across the tile. You must be careful, of course, not to leave the flame in any one spot, and you must not overheat. If you want a less hazardous method, you can place aluminum foil over the square and use a warm iron. Press the edges of the loose tile with the iron, and then place weights over the tile to press it in place until the mastic sets up fully.

2. If there seems to be insufficient mastic to glue the tile back down, apply heat again and peel back the edges. Then clean out the old mastic as completely as you can. Apply new floor tile mastic, but be careful not to put so much down that mastic will squeeze out when you press down on the tile. Replace the tile

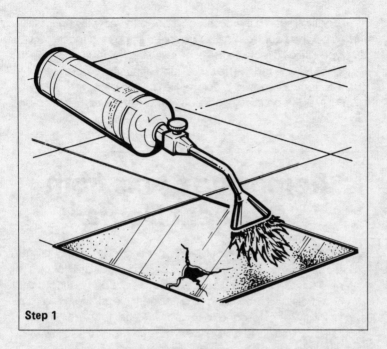

Step 1

and weight it down until the mastic has cured. Check the label for the prescribed drying time.

3. If the tile is botched up and needs to be replaced, you can use either heat or cold to remove the bad tile. If you do not have a propane torch, try placing dry ice or a metal pot filled with ice, water, and ice cream salt over the tile. After about five to ten minutes, the cold will make both the tile and the mastic very brittle, allowing you to flip the tile out in chips with a putty knife. Tap the putty knife with a hammer as you do, and the tile will shatter.

4. Once you remove the tile, clean away all the old mastic. Scraping with a wide putty knife is probably the best way to clean the entire area.

5. Now you are ready to lay the new tile. Place it down in the opening before you apply any mastic. This enables you to match up the pattern. You may find that the new tile does not fit

exactly. If such is the case, sand down the new tile until it fits.

6. Apply the floor tile mastic (be sure it is the kind made for your type of tile) directly to the floor, following the instructions on the label. Now warm the new tile, using either the propane torch or the electric iron, and press the tile firmly in place.

7. Put weights on the tile, and leave them there for the prescribed drying time.

25 Removing Spots from Resilient Floors

THOSE STURDY and beautiful resilient floors that are so popular in modern kitchens and bathrooms receive a great deal of punishment. Although you can usually avoid a stain by treating a spot immediately and then just mopping them clean, there are some stains that will not respond to the mop. Rather than letting such a floor become so unattractive that you must replace it, follow these tips for removing spots from your resilient floor.

HERE IS WHAT YOU WILL NEED

Materials	Tools
☐ All-purpose spray cleaner	☐ Damp cloth
☐ 0000 steel wool	☐ Metal spatula
☐ Liquid wax	☐ Mop
☐ Ice	
☐ Dry cleaner	
☐ Rubbing alcohol	
☐ Ammonia	
☐ Oxalic acid	
☐ Hydrogen peroxide	
☐ White vinegar	

1. Remember, you can prevent spills from turning into stains by treating them immediately. In many cases, a quick wipe with a damp cloth removes the spill and the possibility of a stain.

2. Know the material the flooring is made of; it could be vinyl, asphalt, rubber, or linoleum.

3. Treat heel marks, probably the most common problem, with an all-purpose spray cleaner. If the cleaner fails to get rid of the marks, use 0000 steel wool dipped into liquid wax. Then go over the area with a damp cloth. When dry, wax the floor.

4. Tar, chewing gum or candle wax will get brittle if you hold an ice cube against the substance. Then use a metal spatula or some other such dull tool to scrape away the brittle matter. If there is residue left, try a dry cleaner and 0000 steel wool. Wash the area, and wax it when dry.

5. Ink stains should be covered for a few minutes with a rubbing alcohol compress. Then—unless the floor is linoleum—wipe the area with an ammonia dampened rag.

6. You can often scrape up paint spots and spatters with a spatula. If not, try wearing them away with 0000 steel wool and liquid wax.

7. Rust stains should be treated by rubbing on a dilute solution of oxalic acid with 0000 steel wool. Oxalic acid is available at paint stores, but you must observe all the caution notices when using it on your floors.

8. Mustard will sometimes leave a stain if allowed to dry. After removing all the dried matter with a spatula or damp cloth, make a compress soaked with hydrogen peroxide and leave it on the stain for several minutes. Then wash, let dry, and wax.

9. Drain and toilet bowl cleaners are caustics and should be neutralized with white vinegar as soon as possible. Wash, let dry, and wax.

10. Fruit stains and coffee stains that you cannot wipe up should first be rubbed with 0000 steel wool and liquid wax. Then, remove all the wax and make a compress soaked with hydrogen peroxide. Leave the compress on for several minutes. Wash, let dry, and wax.

26 How to Remove Cigarette Burns from a Carpet

CIGARETTE BURNS in carpeting are unsightly, and although you cannot repair the damage completely without having the carpet rewoven, there are several ways to hide the burned spot very effectively. Here are the steps to take.

HERE IS WHAT YOU WILL NEED

Materials	Tools
☐ Carpet scrap	☐ Fingernail scissors
☐ Glue	
☐ Carpet tape	

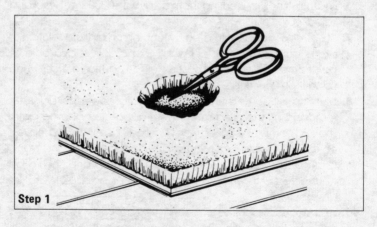

Step 1

1. Use a pair of fingernail scissors to clip away all the blackened fibers. If the burn failed to go down all the way to the backing, you may not have to do anything else; the one low spot generally is not noticeable. If the burn did go to the backing, however, scrape away the charred matter.

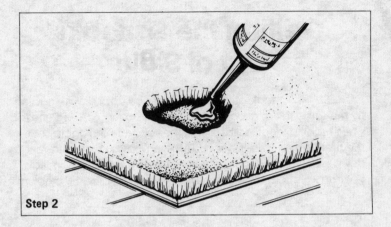

Step 2

2. If the backing shows, clip new fibers from a carpet scrap and glue them in place over the hole. First put glue on the hole, and then as the glue gets tacky enough to support the fibers, carefully place a few of them at a time upright in the glue.

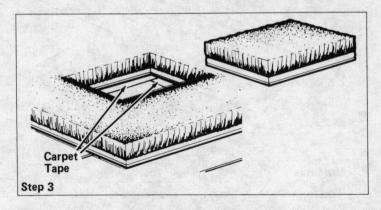

Carpet Tape

Step 3

3. If the damage is more severe, cut an entire square out of the carpet and replace it with a scrap piece. Use carpet tape that is sticky on both sides to hold the patch in place, and make sure that the nap of the new carpet scrap lays the same way as the nap of the carpet already down.

27 Getting the Squeaks Out of Stairs

THE STAIRWAY that squeaks when you walk up or down is caused by the same thing that causes your floor to squeak; two pieces of wood rubbing together. It is usually the tread rubbing against either the riser or the stringer because these boards are not fastened down securely. Stop their movement, and you stop the squeak. If you can work from under the stairs, here is how to cure the problem.

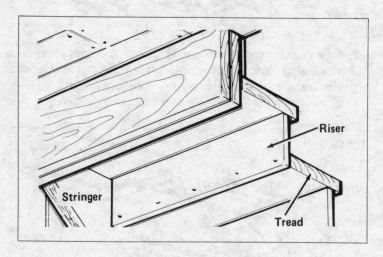

HERE IS WHAT YOU WILL NEED

Materials	Tools
☐ Wooden wedges or blocks	☐ Hammer
☐ White polyvinyl or any wood glue	☐ Nailset
☐ Finishing nails	
☐ Graphite powder or talcum powder	
☐ Wood putty	

1. Have someone walk on the stairs, going back and forth on the step that squeaks, while you try to spot movement from below. Look especially for loose nails, split boards, or anything else that could cause the movement.

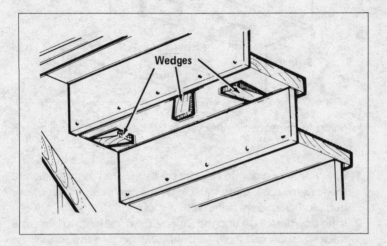

Wedges

2. The best way to stop the movement is to drive wedges between the rubbing members. Cut the wedges from scrap shingles.

3. Coat the wedges with glue (white polyvinyl or any wood glue) on the side that will press against a flat surface.

4. Drive the wedges into the seam, making them go in as tight as possible.

5. When you get them in place, secure the wedges with nails. Use small nails, and blunt the points to avoid splitting the wedges.

6. If the seams are too small to admit wedges, cut wood blocks (1x2s) to fit into the joints under the stairs. Put a coat of glue on the sides that will touch the stairs, and then—as you hold the blocks in place—secure them with nails. Be sure your nails do not go through the stairs and protrude from the top.

If there is no way to work from under the stairs, you have to try to find the movement from topside. Unfortunately, you frequently cannot spot the problem and must guess where the trouble is by

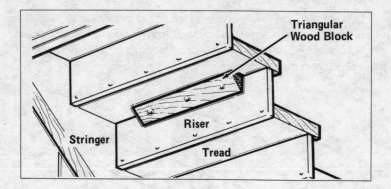

listening to the squeak. After you track down the squeak, here is what to do.

1. Buy a tube of graphite powder and squeeze the graphite into the joints all around the squeak. Or you can use talcum powder in a plastic squeeze bottle with a spout.

2. If the powder fails to stop the squeak, drive finishing nails into the tread at such an angle that they will go into the riser or the stringer where you think the movement is. Use a nailset to sink the heads below the surface, and then cover the holes with wood putty.

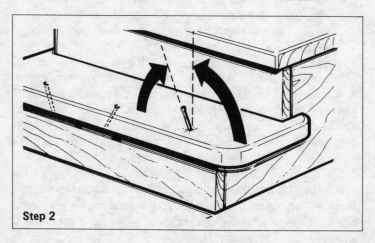

Step 2

Sagging Support Beams **28**

MANY TIMES, a cracked wall or a sticking door upstairs—or even a roof leak—is actually caused by a problem in the basement. The problem is that the joists under the first floor are sagging. Once the joists give a little, the sag continues on up the line. Before you start trying to remedy the results upstairs, therefore, you need to take care of the cause in the basement. Although the cure is simple, you first must check your local building code to see that what you do conforms to the law. Once you get that aspect of the problem cleared up, just follow these steps to remedy your sagging supports.

HERE IS WHAT YOU WILL NEED

Materials	Tools
☐ Nails	☐ Screw jack
☐ 4x4s	☐ Saw
☐ Steel columns or adjustable jack posts	☐ Hammer
	☐ Measuring tape
☐ Concrete mix	☐ Carpenter's level
	☐ Chisel
	☐ Trowel

1. Buy or rent a screw-type house jack (commonly called a *screw jack*).
2. Place a 4x4 timber directly under the center of the sag to serve as a support base for the screw jack.
3. Cut another 4x4 timber to run across the sagging joists and beyond to several nonsagging joists on either side. Nail this beam in place across the joists.
4. Place the screw jack on the support base.
5. Measure from the top of the lowered screw jack to the bottom of the beam you nailed up and cut a third 4x4 to this length.
6. Install this third piece as a vertical between the jack and the beam. Since it must be plumb, use a level to set it.
7. Turn the handle of the screw jack until you feel resistance, and **STOP**. The leveling process must be very gradual; otherwise,

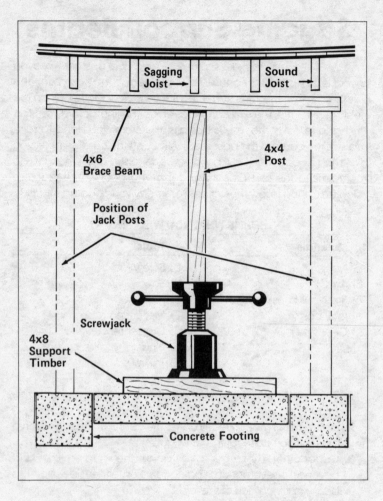

Sagging Joist →

Sound Joist →

4x6 Brace Beam

4x4 Post

Position of Jack Posts

Screwjack

4x8 Support Timber

Concrete Footing

you can crack your walls and do great damage to the house.

8. Wait a full 24 hours, and then turn the screw jack handle only one quarter of a turn. The handle will probably be very easy to turn, and you will be tempted to turn more, but be patient. Continue to make no more than a quarter turn every 24 hours. If you miss a day do not compensate for it with additional turning.

9. When the sagging beams begin to straighten out, start checking them with your level every day.

10. When they are all level, install columns at each end of each beam to secure them. You can buy steel Lally columns or you can cut 4x4s; there are also adjustable jack posts that work like the screw jack and are the easiest supports to set.

11. No matter what kind of supports you decide to install, you must make sure that the footing below is sound. The common concrete basement floor is not reliable enough. You should remove a two-foot section of the old floor where each support post will go, pour a concrete footing that is at least a foot thick, and make it level with the rest of the floor. When it has cured, you can put the support posts on the footing and know that the floor will not give way.

Installing Wallboard 29

IF YOU EVER decide to finish a room with exposed studs, the easiest way to accomplish the task is to attach wallboard to the studs. After the wallboard is up, you can paint, paper, or texture it. Wallboard (also known as Sheetrock™, plasterboard, drywall, and gypsum board) possesses excellent insulating and sound deadening qualities.

Although it is a snap to figure how much wallboard to buy (just compute the square footage of the walls and ceiling), it takes some planning to end up with as few joints as possible. The standard size sheets for walls are 4x8 feet. You normally place them with the long side running from floor to ceiling, but you can place them horizontally if by doing so you eliminate a joint. You can buy longer sized sheets for the ceiling. All wallboard sheets are four feet wide, but most lumberyards offer 12 foot lengths.

As to the number of nails, rolls of tape, and the amount of joint compound you will need, consult the table at your local lumberyard to learn how much of each is required for the square footage involved. For example, 1000 square feet of ½-inch thick wallboard (the most popular home thickness) requires about 5¼ pounds of coated nails, a five-gallon pail of joint compound in mixed form, and a 500-foot roll of tape. Each outside corner requires a metal cornerbead.

Once you buy all the materials you need for the project, just follow these steps to install your new wallboard walls.

HERE IS WHAT YOU WILL NEED

Materials	Tools
☐ Wallboard sheets	☐ Measuring tape
☐ Coated nails	☐ Hammer
☐ Joint tape	☐ Wallboard knife
☐ Joint compound	☐ Straightedge
☐ Metal cornerbeads	☐ Sawhorse or other support
☐ 2x4s	☐ Sanding block
☐ Wooden boards	☐ Drill
☐ Sandpaper	☐ Keyhole saw
☐ Molding and baseboards	☐ Putty knife
☐ Sealer or primer	☐ Metal float
☐ Paint	☐ Paintbrush

1. Install the ceilings first. If possible, try to span the entire width with a single sheet of wallboard to reduce the number of joints. Before you can work on the ceilings, though, you need to construct a pair of T-braces from 2x4s about an inch longer than the distance from floor to ceiling. Nail lighter boards about three feet long to the 2x4s to form the Ts, and then position and wedge the braces against the wallboard sheet to hold it in place until you finish nailing.

2. Drive nails at seven-inch intervals into all the joints covered by the sheet. Start in the center of the wallboard panel and work out.

3. After you drive in each nail, give it one extra hammer blow to dimple the surface slightly. Take care, though, not to break the face paper.

4. When you need to cut panels to complete the coverage, use a

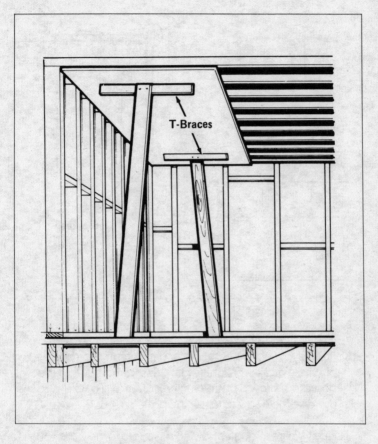

T-Braces

wallboard knife along a straightedge. All you want to do with the knife is cut the face paper. After you make the cut, place the board over the edge of a sawhorse (or some other type of support) and bend it down. The gypsum core will snap along the line you cut. Then turn the panel over, cut the paper on the other side, and smooth the rough edges with a very coarse sanding block.

5. When the ceiling is finished, put up the walls. Again space the nails seven inches apart, but start nailing seven inches from the ceiling. Butt the wall panels against the ceiling sheets.

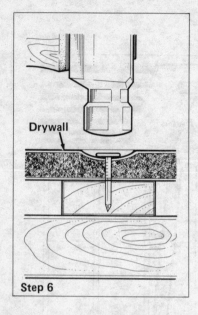

Drywall

Step 6

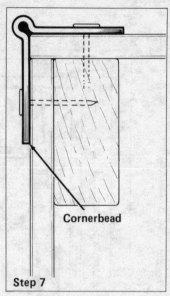

Cornerbead

Step 7

6. Dimple all nails.

7. If outside corners are involved, nail the cornerbeads in place.

8. Be sure to measure carefully for any cutouts such as electrical outlets, switches, or light fixtures. To make cutouts in the wallboard, first draw a pattern of the cutout, drill a hole, and then use a keyhole saw to follow the pattern around.

Once you are through applying the board to the walls, you face the problem of covering up all the nails and joints. This is where you use the joint compound and the tape in a technique called *taping and bedding.*

1. Use a wide putty knife to spread joint compound into the slight recess created by the tapered edges of the wallboard sheets. Smooth the compound until it is even with the rest of the surface.

2. Next, center the wallboard tape over the joint and press it firmly into the compound. Since some compound will squeeze out,

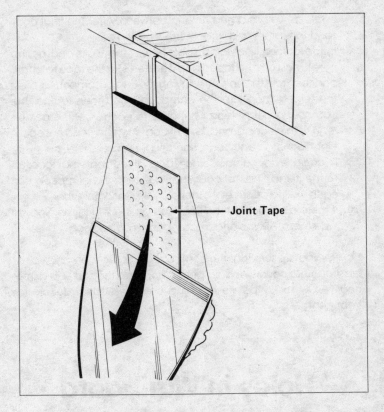

Joint Tape

you should make sure that there is still a good bed underneath.

3. When you get the tape imbedded into the compound all along the joint, smooth it with your putty knife.

4. When the compound is completely dry (usually 24 hours later), apply a second very thin coat of compound that extends out a few inches to either side of the first coat.

5. After the second coat dries complete, apply a third coat, extending it out to about six inches to either side. A metal float will do better than the putty knife at this stage.

6. When the third coat is dry, feather all the edges with a sanding block covered with medium grit sandpaper.

7. Fill all the dimples with compound. They also require three coats as well as drying time in between. After the final coat, sand to feather and smooth the dimpled spots.

8. Inside corners, including spots where the walls and ceiling meet, must also be taped and bedded. Cut the tape to length and then fold it in half. After laying the bed of compound, press the folded tape into the compound and then feather the compound out at least 1½ inches to each side. The corners require three coats, and the last coat should extend out about eight inches to each side. Sanding is required here,too.

9. If you have any outside corners, apply three coats that taper up to the bead. The last coat should extend the compound on each wall to about eight inches wide. Sand here,too.

10. If there are cracks at the floor and ceiling, install moldings to hide them. Always attach baseboards at the floor.

After you are sure that the compound is completely dry, wait at least another couple of days before applying the sealer or primer coat. Allow to dry before applying any subsequent decorative treatment.

30   Holes in Wallboard

THE EASE AND economy of dry wall construction are marred only by the fact that wallboard can develop holes the first time someone slams a doorknob against it. These holes may look like complete disasters, but you will be amazed at how easily you can patch them. Small holes require one kind of backing, while larger ones may necessitate another. First, here is what to do for the smaller hole that needs a backing for a patch.

HERE IS WHAT YOU WILL NEED

Materials	Tools
☐ Tin can lid	☐ Keyhole saw

Materials	Tools
☐ Wire	☐ Wire cutters or scissors
☐ Wooden stick	☐ Brush or trowel
☐ Spackling compound	☐ Screwdriver
☐ Primer	
☐ Paint	
☐ Scrap wallboard	
☐ Wooden board	
☐ Countersunk screws	

1. Remove any loose material around the hole.
2. Select a tin can lid that is bigger than the hole and measure across the lid. Then use a keyhole saw to cut a slit extending out from both sides of the hole so that you can slip the lid into the hole sideways.
3. Punch two holes in the center of the lid and run a wire through them.
4. Now slip the lid through the slit, holding onto the wire. With the lid inside, pull the wire until the lid is flat against the inside of the wall.
5. Twist the wire around a stick that is long enough to span the hole. This technique will hold the lid in place.
6. You can now plaster over the hole with spackling compound (available at paint or hardware stores in either ready mixed or powdered form). Cover all of the backing plate, the slit, and the edges, but resist trying to make the main body of the patch level with the rest of the wall.
7. When the first patch dries, remove the stick and snip the wire off flush with the patch.
8. Apply a second coat of spackling compound, bringing the surface up level with the rest of the wall. This coat will, of course, cover the remaining tip of wire.
9. Use a brush or trowel to texture the patch so that it matches the rest of the wall.
10. Let the patch dry overnight before applying the primer coat for repainting.

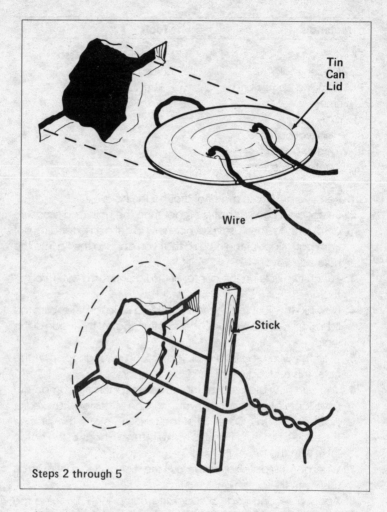

Tin
Can
Lid

Wire

Stick

Steps 2 through 5

Now, here is how to take care of those bigger patches. Rather than applying many layers of the compound to patch, you should insert a scrap of wallboard into the hole.

1. Cut a scrap piece of wallboard into a square that is slightly larger than the hole.

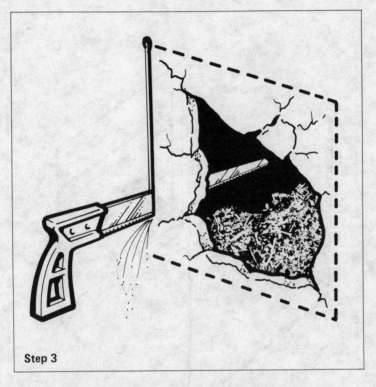

Step 3

2. Lay the wallboard over the hole and trace around it.
3. Use a keyhole saw to cut along the pattern you just traced.
4. Now you need backing. Select a board about six inches longer than the widest span of the hole you just cut.
5. Slip the backing board into the hole, and hold it firmly against the inside of the wallboard.
6. Insert countersunk screws through the wall and into the backing on each side of the hole to hold the backing securely against the inside of the wall. Keep turning the screws until the flat heads dig down below the surface.
7. Now spread all four edges of the patch with spackling compound or joint compound, and spread compound over the back of the patch where it will rest against the backing board.

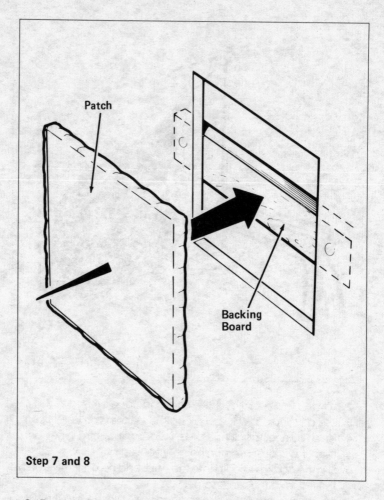

Patch

Backing
Board

Step 7 and 8

8. Ease the patch into place, and hold it there until the compound starts to set up.

9. When the compound is dry, fill up the slits around the patch. Then cover the entire patch—plus the screw heads—with spackling, using a brush or trowel to make the compound match the texture of the rest of the wall.

10. Let the entire area dry; then prime and repaint.

Panel a Wall

31

THE LARGE selection in wall paneling makes it possible to achieve almost any effect you want in a room. You can purchase actual plywood paneling either finished or unfinished, or you can buy hardboard panels in finishes ranging from barn siding to marble. The plastic-coated finishes on both hardboard and plywood panels are almost impervious to scratches and stains, and they are entirely washable as long as you do not drown them. Just go over the finish with a damp cloth and detergent.

The ease with which the panels go up makes paneling a wall a simple do-it-yourself project. Modern adhesives virtually eliminate nailing, and the preparation and basic installation steps are the same for both plywood and hardboard.

HERE IS WHAT YOU WILL NEED

Materials	Tools
☐ Plywood or hardboard paneling	☐ Plane
	☐ Putty knife
☐ Plywood or gypsum board backing	☐ Screwdriver
	☐ Hammer
☐ Shims	☐ Measuring tape
☐ Long straight board	☐ Level
☐ Drywall compound	☐ Scribing compass
☐ Sandpaper	☐ Saber saw or coping saw
☐ Furring strips	☐ Caulking gun
☐ Nails	☐ Padded block
☐ Shingles	☐ Scissors
☐ Polyethylene vapor barrier	☐ Crosscut handsaw or power saw
☐ Moldings	
☐ Panel adhesive	☐ Drill
☐ Tape	☐ Keyhole saw
☐ Wood putty	☐ Miter box
	☐ Nailset

1. You could actually apply panels directly to the studs where you

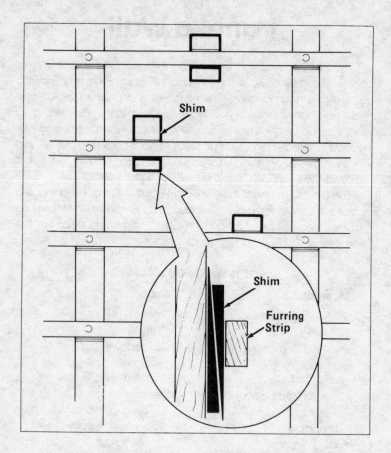

Shim

Shim

Furring
Strip

have new construction, but since the panels tend to give a little and are far from soundproof, it is best to provide either a plywood or gypsum board backing. Nevertheless, if you decide to apply paneling directly to the studs, make sure that the studs are free of high or low spots. Plane away any high spots and attach shims to compensate for low spots.

2. Remove the molding and trim from existing walls and check for highs and lows by drawing a long straight board across the wall and watching for any gaps as it moves across. Build up the lows with drywall compound, and sand down the high spots. If the walls are badly cracked or extremely uneven, you should install furring strips.

3. Masonry walls must always be furred and waterproofed. Furring strips are actually slats of wood (1x2s or 1x3s) nailed to the wall. Nail the furring horizontally on 16-inch centers, starting at the floor and finishing at the ceiling. Place short vertical strips between the horizontals, spacing them every four feet so that they will come under the joints between the panels. Nail furring strips to the wall with masonry nails, compensating for lows by wedging shingles under the strips. A four mil polyethylene vapor barrier should be placed over the furring of masonry walls and on any other type of walls where moisture might be a problem.

4. Remember that you must compensate for the increased thickness of the wall at electrical switches and wall outlets. Remove the plates and reset the boxes out the necessary distance.

5. Allow the paneling to stabilize to the moisture content of the room before you begin attaching it to the walls. Stack the panels with strips of boards between each one, and then leave them there for at least two days. This step is very important for a successful paneling job.

6. When the panels are ready to go, lean them against the wall as you think they should be placed. This gives you a chance to match the wood graining in the most pleasing manner. When you have them the way you want them, be sure to number the panels.

7. Measure the distance from floor to ceiling at several different points. If the panels have to be cut for height, you can cut all of them the same, provided that there is no more than ¼ inch variance. If there is more variance than ¼ inch, you should measure the height for each panel and cut it to fit. If you are not going to use a ceiling molding, each panel must be cut to conform to the ceiling line, but if you do use ceiling moldings— and you should—leave ¼ inch gap at the top. There also needs to be ¼ inch gap at the floor that will be covered by the floor molding.

8. Since very few corners are plumb, place the first panel that is to

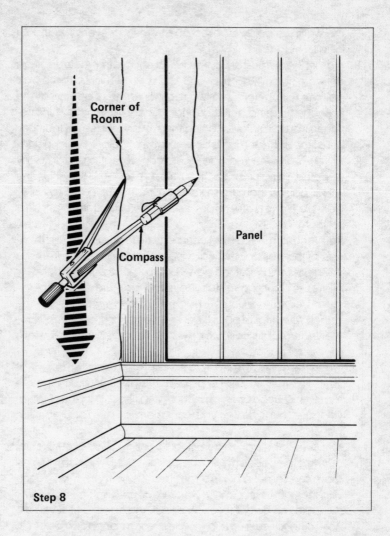

Corner of
Room

Compass

Panel

Step 8

go in a corner next to the wall and check the plumb with a
level. Get the panel plumb and close enough to the corner so
that you can span the space with a scribing compass. Then run
the compass down the corner, with the point in the corner and
the pencil marking a line on the panel. Cut the panel along

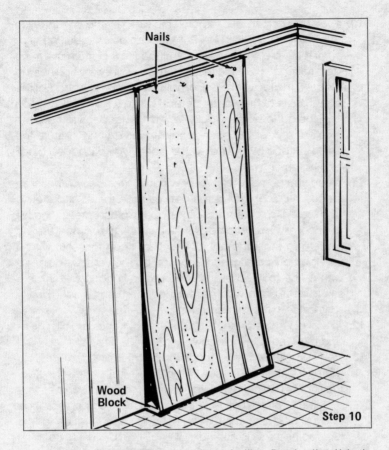

Nails

Wood
Block

Step 10

the line with a saber saw equipped with a fine-toothed blade
or with a coping saw.

9. If instead of cementing the panels you plan to nail them, use
the nails made by the paneling manufacturer. You can use 2d
(1 inch) finishing nails to attach the panels to furring strips, but if
you must go through a wall to reach the studs, be sure to use
nails long enough to penetrate about an inch into the studs.
Drive the nails every six inches along the edges and about
every twelve inches through the center. Check frequently to
make sure you are hitting the furring strips.

10. If you are using mastic to panel the wall, get the kind that you apply with a caulking gun. Run a ribbon across all furring strips or—if there are no strips—in about the same pattern as if there were furring strips. Place the panel against the wall and nail it in place at the top with a pair of nails. Then pull the bottom of the panel out from the wall and prop it with a scrap block of wood until the adhesive gets tacky. When this happens, remove the block and press the panel against the wall. Then secure the entire surface by pounding the panel with a padded block and hammer.

11. When you come to a door or window, take one of the large pieces of paper that came between the sheets of paneling and use it as a pattern. Tape the paper in place, press it against the door or window frame and then cut it with a scissors. Use this pattern to mark the panel, which you can then cut with a fine-toothed crosscut handsaw or with a power saw equipped with a fine-toothed blade. When using a handsaw or table saw, cut the panel with the face up. When using a hand power saw, cut with the face down.

12. To make cutouts for electrical outlets or switches, drill pilot holes and then use a keyhole saw.

13. Next comes the finishing touch that will hide any and all of your mistakes—the application of molding. Most panel manufacturers offer prefinished moldings to match. You can get floor moldings, ceiling moldings, inside or outside corner moldings, and just about anything else you need. Use a miter box and a fine-toothed saw to cut the moldings, and be sure to countersink the nails with a nailset and fill the holes with matching wood putty.

32 Covering Walls with Fabric

IF PAINTING sounds too messy and wallpapering is more work

than you care to tackle, you should consider covering your walls with fabric. Before you decide that such a project is restricted to the professionals, just look at these simple steps.

HERE IS WHAT YOU WILL NEED

Materials	Tools
☐ Fabric	☐ Plumb bob chalk line
☐ Staples	☐ Scissors
☐ Shirtboard	☐ Staple gun
☐ Glue	
☐ Molding strips	

1. Select fabric in rolls as wide as possible. Remember when picking a pattern that the panels must match adjacent panels.
2. Since it is unlikely that the last panel will match the first one after you go all around the room, pick out the most obscure corner in which to start.
3. Use a plumb bob chalk line as a guide for getting the first panel straight up and down.
4. Cut each panel to the height of the room plus one inch extra at both top and bottom.
5. Take the first panel, turn an inch of fabric under at the top, and staple the top of the panel to the wall so that the side edge lines up with the chalk line. Unless you plan to cover the top and bottom with molding or ribbon, place the staples as near and as in line with the ceiling as possible. Try to use only as many staples as are required to prevent the fabric from sagging; you can also run a bead of glue across the top to guard against sagging.
6. Staple down both sides of the first panel about ¼ inch in from the edges.
7. Fold the inch under at the bottom, pull the fabric tight, and staple the panel along the baseboard.
8. For the second panel, place the edge face to face with the first panel. In other words, the reverse side of the second panel faces out.

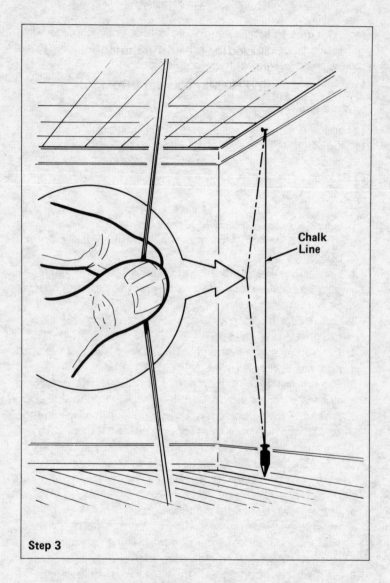

Step 3

9. Staple the second panel at several spots about ½ inch in from where the edges of the two panels meet lengthwise.

10. Now staple strips of cardboard (½-inch wide) all along the edges you just stapled together. Make sure that the cardboard strips are straight.

11. When you pull the second panel of fabric over into position, you will find you have a hidden seam that is stapled securely in place.

12. Staple down the other edge about ¼ inch in from the edge.

13. Repeat the same procedure as you continue on around the room.

14. Rough cut the panels for doors and windows, turning the excess under and stapling them as close to the frames as possible. Keep the number of staples to a minimum, using glue wherever possible. With some fabrics, you can glue the entire job.

15. Turn under and glue the last panel in place over the staples you left showing along the edge of the first panel.

16. If you wish to hide the staples at the top and bottom, you can glue a band of the fabric—or even a wide contrasting ribbon—around these seams. You can also attach molding strips to cover the staples.

Replacing Damaged Molding

33

MOLDING IS ALMOST a panacea for botched-up wall seams and joints. Of course, it can be decorative as well, but generally its main function is to hide cracks. When the molding itself gets damaged, however, you cannot hide the problem; you must replace at least a section of the molding and perhaps the entire piece. Since the most easily damaged moldings are the baseboards—down where they can be hit by all sorts of things—the following instructions describe how to replace baseboard molding, but you can apply the same technique to other moldings in other places.

HERE IS WHAT YOU WILL NEED

Materials	Tools
☐ Wooden wedges	☐ Putty knife
☐ Replacement moldings	☐ Screwdriver
☐ Finishing nails	☐ Wood block
☐ Paint	☐ Pry bar
	☐ Hammer
	☐ Pliers
	☐ Miter box
	☐ Backsaw or hacksaw
	☐ Coping saw
	☐ Nailset
	☐ Paintbrush

Shoe Molding

Putty Knife

Step 1

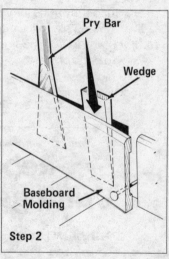

Pry Bar

Wedge

Baseboard Molding

Step 2

1. First, you must remove any shoe molding, the quarter-round piece that fits against both the baseboard and the floor. Since it is nailed to the subfloor, apply gentle prying pressure with a putty knife at one end of the shoe molding to get it started. Then you can use a screwdriver with a wood block for leverage. Once started, the shoe molding should come up fairly easily. Try not to be too rough, though, or you can break it, adding to your replacement costs and troubles.

2. Next, pry out the damaged baseboard. Start at one end, inserting a small flat pry bar between the baseboard and the wall. Pry gently, and move farther down the line whenever you can, slipping small wooden wedges in the gaps. Work all the way along the baseboard prying and wedging. Then work back between the wedges, tapping the wedges in deeper as the baseboard comes out more. The baseboard soon will come off.

3. Check to see if any nails pulled through either the shoe molding or the baseboard, and if so, pull out the nails completely.

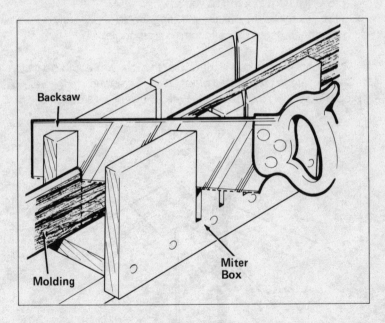

If the old baseboard came out intact, you can use it as a pattern for cutting the new one. If part is missing or if it is badly damaged, however, you must cut the new moldings to fit without the aid of a pattern. You will need a miter box to cut the moldings; an inexpensive wooden miter box will be adequate for this work. The slots allow you to cut 45-degree angles, and you should use either a backsaw or a fine blade in a hacksaw. Be sure to place the molding you are about to cut next to the molding against which it will rest in order to make certain that the cut you plan to make is the right one. Then follow these instructions to cut the new molding.

1. Place a scrap of wood in the miter box.
2. Make sure that the lip of the miter box presses against the edge of a table or bench so that you can hold it steady.
3. Hold the molding tightly against the side of the miter box to prevent it from slipping as you saw.
4. After you make the cut, the molding should fit perfectly against the other mitered piece to form a right angle.

If you need an inside right angle, though, you could go crazy trying to get the two angled pieces to fit. The solution to this vexing problem is called a coped joint. Here is how you make such a joint.

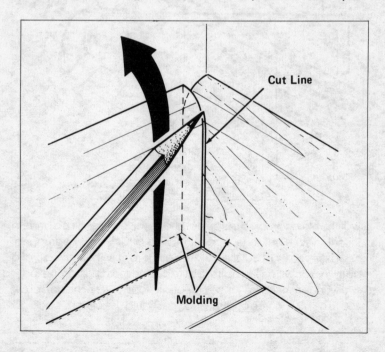

Cut Line

Molding

1. Cut one piece of baseboard to fit precisely in the space.
2. Lay this piece of baseboard flat on the floor with its backside facing up.
3. Place another piece of baseboard molding down against the back of the piece on the floor. The tapered end of the top molding should point to the edge of the bottom piece. If it does not, turn the top piece end for end. Now it is in place.
4. Trace the contour of the top piece onto the bottom piece.
5. Use a coping saw to cut along the pattern.
6. When cut, the two pieces will fit closely together to form a false miter—referred to as a coped joint—that creates a perfect inside corner.

When you finish all the mitering and coped joints, you are ready to install the new baseboard molding and reinstall the shoe molding.

1. Fit all the pieces together before nailing to make sure that you cut them correctly.
2. Nail the baseboards in place with finishing nails. Then use a nailset to drive the nail heads below the surface of the molding.
3. Reinstall the shoe molding with finishing nails as well. Remember, shoe molding must be nailed to the floor and not to the baseboard. Drive the nail heads below the surface of the shoe molding with a nailset.
4. Paint all new moldings to match the color of your walls.

Replacing a Ceramic Tile 34

GENERALLY, the hardest part about replacing a cracked ceramic tile is finding a new tile that matches. Some colors are not easy to find. If your tile is very old, you may have to go to a wrecking yard to find a match. Once you have the right tile, however, just follow these directions for removing the cracked one and putting in its replacement.

HERE IS WHAT YOU WILL NEED

Materials	Tools
☐ Replacement tile	☐ Power drill with carbide tip
☐ Tile mastic	☐ Glass cutter
☐ Tape or wooden toothpicks	☐ Cold chisel
☐ Tile grout	☐ Hammer
☐ Sponge	☐ Putty knife
☐ Terry cloth towel	☐ Safety goggles

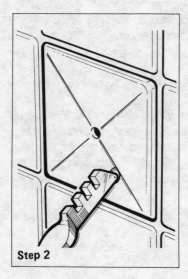

Step 2

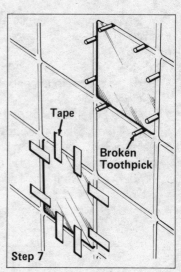

Tape

Broken
Toothpick

Step 7

1. The best method for removing the old tile is to drill a hole in its middle with a carbide bit in your power drill.
2. Next, score an "X" in the tile with a glass cutter.
3. Take a cold chisel and hammer, and break away the tile without damaging any of the surrounding tiles. Wear safety goggles to prevent eye injury.
4. Clean the bed on which the old tile rested, removing all the

bumps to make the surface as smooth as possible. Then remove any loose grout around the opening.

5. Purchase tile mastic at a hardware store, and spread it over the back of the new tile. Keep the mastic about a half inch away from all four edges.

6. Hold the tile by its edges and ease it into place. Press until the new tile is flush with the surrounding tiles.

7. Position the tile to provide an even space all around it, and then either tape it in place or insert broken toothpicks to keep gravity from pulling the tile down before the mastic sets up.

8. Allow enough time for the mastic to cure, and then mix tile grout according to the directions on the package. Be sure to mix the grout until it is completely smooth.

9. Fill in the space all the way around the tile with the grout mix. Dip either a sponge or your finger into the mix, and apply it so as to fill the space entirely. You will do no harm if you get the grout on other tiles.

10. After the grout has set for about 15 minutes, take a damp terry cloth towel and gently remove any excess on the other tiles. Just be careful not to dig out any of the grout from between the tiles.

11. Wait until the next day, and then rub the damp towel more vigorously to remove all traces of grout and to polish the tile. If the tile you replaced is in a shower, make sure that you avoid getting any water on it until the grout has set up completely.

Mildew

35

EVEN THE NICEST homes can have mildew, an ugly-looking mess that can also produce an unpleasant odor. Mildew is a fungus that floats in the air until it finds the right conditions to start growing on the wall. What are those conditions? Mildew spores must have moisture and dirt to feed on. The bathroom walls, of course, are among the most common places for mildew to settle, but you can get rid of the fungus easily if you follow these simple steps.

HERE IS WHAT YOU WILL NEED

Materials	Tools
☐ Household bleach	☐ Toothbrush
☐ Plastic squeeze bottle	☐ Stiff brush or broom
☐ Household ammonia	☐ Garden hose
☐ Trisodium phosphate	
☐ Powdered detergent	

1. Cover all the mildew spots you can see with household bleach. Since most of the fungus will be along the grout lines between tiles or in corners, a good way to apply the bleach is with a

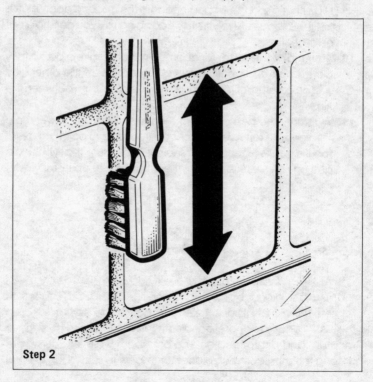

Step 2

plastic squeeze bottle (such as a shampoo or dish detergent bottle). Be sure to observe all of the caution notices on the bleach bottle regarding dangers to your skin and respiratory system.

2. Most of the mildew spots will disappear in a few minutes, but stubborn spots may need additional bleach and perhaps a light scrubbing. An old toothbrush is ideal for scrubbing between tiles and in the corners.

3. When all the mildew is gone, rinse all the bleach away with water.

4. When you are sure that none of the bleach remains on the walls, wash the walls with household ammonia. **REMEMBER: YOU MUST NEVER MIX BLEACH AND AMMONIA.** The combination releases potentially fatal chlorine gas. The ammonia will kill the spores of the fungus, preventing the mildew from making a speedy return.

Of course, new mildew can get started unless you eliminate the conditions that allow it to thrive. Find out what is causing the excess moisture. If the mildew occurs in a bath, kitchen, or laundry room, you know where the moisture comes from, and your problem then is to discover a way to exhaust the excess moisture. A dehumidifier or an exhaust fan may be the answer, or regular airing of the room may do the job. If the moisture comes from a leak under the house or bad drainage, you must correct the problem to eliminate your mildew problem for good. Naturally, it is always a good idea to keep walls free of dirt, grease, and soap scum.

Mildew also forms outside. Many people think that they can kill the fungus when they paint their homes with a mildew-retardant paint. Usually, however, they see the mildew growing back through the paint in a matter of weeks. No paint can kill mildew; you must kill mildew before painting. Here is how to get rid of fungus from exterior walls. Mix ⅔ cup TSP (trisodium phosphate—available at most paint stores), ⅓ cup powdered detergent, and one quart liquid household bleach. Add enough warm water to make one gallon of solution, and scrub the affected areas with a stiff brush or broom; then hose them off. Be sure to trim back trees and bushes that prevent air and sunlight from reaching mildew-prone areas.

36

Papering a Wall

WALL COVERINGS can make a dramatic difference in a room's appearance. Vinyl wall coverings are the most popular because they are washable, fade resistant, and most are strippable. That last advantage looms large when you have to recover the walls later on. Strippable coverings can be peeled off the wall all in one piece, eliminating messy steaming, soaking, and scraping. Prepasted coverings are also very popular because they are easy to use and less messy than unpasted coverings. Prepastes require the use of a water box to activate the paste. If you select a covering that is not prepasted, you must be sure to use the prescribed type of paste. If you are applying a vinyl covering, for example, use one of the special vinyl adhesives that are much stronger and mildew resistant than the wheat paste.

Figuring how many rolls to buy is strictly a mathematical exercise, but you have to know the rules. No matter how wide the roll is, any wall covering roll contains approximately 36 square feet. A roll 24 inches wide is 18 feet long, while a roll that is 27 inches wide is only 16 feet long. Because of trim and waste, though, you can never use all 36 square feet on a roll. The actual yield is usually only about 30 square feet. To figure how many rolls you will need, measure the perimeter of the room and multiply that figure by the room's height. That gives you the square footage. Deduct one roll for every two openings—such as doors and windows—and then apply the yield of 30 square feet against the total. The final figure is the number of rolls to order.

Now you are ready to start to work. But the first thing to do is prepare—not paper—the surface.

HERE IS WHAT YOU WILL NEED

Materials	Tools
☐ Wall covering	☐ Measuring tape
☐ Adhesive (if wall covering is not prepasted)	☐ Steamer
	☐ Putty knife

Materials	Tools
☐ Sandpaper	☐ Chalked plumb line
☐ Spackling	☐ Scissors
☐ Sizing	☐ Water box
	☐ Paintbrush
	☐ Sponge or smoothing brush
	☐ Roller
	☐ Razor blade (with safety edge)

1. A paper wall covering can be applied over old paper, provided that the old covering is sound. If it is not sound, remove any spots of loose paper and feather the edges. If there are more than two layers of old paper, or if you are applying a vinyl wall covering, you should remove all of the old covering. Removing old paper is no easy job, however. You can rent a steamer from the wallpaper store, but you still have to scrape off most of the covering with a wide putty knife.

2. An unpapered wall that is textured should be sanded to remove all the bumps. You need not sand it as slick as glass, but you must get most of the bumps off. Remove the gloss from any enameled surfaces.

3. Fill all cracks and holes.

4. Apply sizing (a sort of glue) over the wall. Absolutely necessary on new wallboard, unpainted plaster, and other such surfaces that would absorb paste, sizing also works well on most other surfaces. Talk to your wallpaper dealer; they can tell you which sizing is compatible with the adhesive you are using.

5. Now you are ready for papering. Select the most inconspicuous corner in the room, and measure out along the wall adjacent to that corner a distance one inch less than the width of your roll.

6. Drop a chalked plumb line from that point, and snap it to show the true vertical. A plumb line is nothing more than a string with a weight on one end. Tack the chalk-coated string at the ceiling so that the weight almost touches the floor. When the weight stops moving, the string is vertical. Hold the bottom end

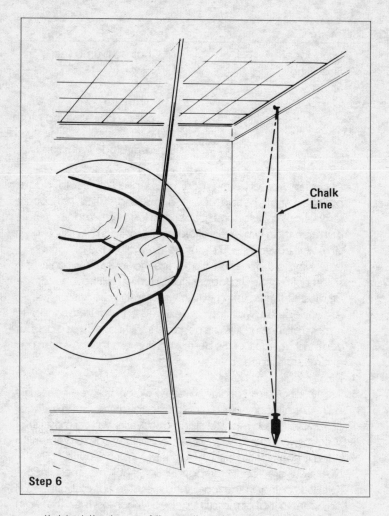

Chalk
Line

Step 6

tight at the base of the wall and snap the string to place a vertical chalk line on the wall.

7. Now you are ready to put up your first strip of paper. Measure the height of the wall, and cut your strip about four inches longer.

8. If you have the prepaste type of wall covering, put the rolled-up strip in the water tray and leave it there for the prescribed amount of time. If you must apply the paste yourself, put the strip face down on a large table and start brushing on the paste at the top. Cover the top half, and then fold the top over—paste against paste—making sure not to crimp or crease the paper. Do the bottom half and fold it over the same way. This technique allows you to carry and work with the strip without getting the paste all over you.

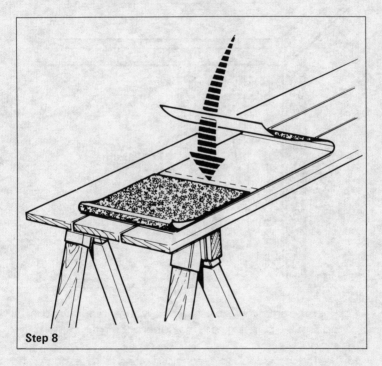

Step 8

9. When you get to the corner, unfold the top half of the paper strip, position the edge next to the chalk line, and be sure it lines up. This step is very important. If the first strip does not line up, the whole room will be out of line. Leave about half the extra four inches of length sticking out at the ceiling. Start smoothing over toward the corner, using your hand, and work over the entire

top half. When you get to the corner, you will find that an extra inch of wall covering remains; take the extra amount around the corner and stick it to the other wall.

10. When the top half is smooth, unfold the bottom half and apply it the same way.

11. Use a sponge or smoothing brush to force out excess paste and air bubbles. Always work toward the edges.

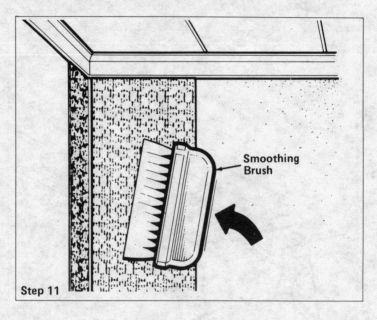

Smoothing Brush

Step 11

12. Hold the smoothing brush vertically, and actually pound it against the corner to push the paper back in the corner until it sticks.

13. Use the same pounding technique along the baseboard and at the ceiling. Do not trim the top and bottom yet.

14. Now unroll some new paper, and make sure it lines up according to the pattern before you cut the second panel.

15. After you prepare the second panel for hanging, place it right next to the first, and then slide it over to butt against the edge.

16. Roll the seams after you smooth each panel.

17. Wait until after you put up and smooth the next panel before trimming the previous one. Use a sharp razor blade, and change blades when you start to notice the blade getting dull.
18. Continue on all the way around the room. Do not skip any areas around doors or windows.
19. When you come to doors and windows, hold the strip over the door and use a hard object to crease an outline of the frame in the wall covering. Then trim the panel to fit, and paste it in place. You can trim it more precisely with a razor blade later.

Repairing Wallpaper **37**

AFTER YOUR wallpaper has been up for a while, you may notice some problems. If not remedied, a loose seam, a slight tear, or a bubble will surely become bigger and more unsightly. When you think back to what you went through in putting the paper up originally, you will certainly prefer to repair rather than to repaper.

HERE IS WHAT YOU WILL NEED

Materials	Tools
☐ Wallpaper paste	☐ Small artist's brush
☐ Vinyl-to-vinyl paste	☐ Seam roller
☐ Razor blades (with safety edge)	
☐ Pin	

1. You can simply repaste seams that come unstuck. Save a small container of the paste for that purpose, and squirt a bit under the loose flaps or spread it on with a small artist's brush. Then use a seam roller to press the paper back down.
2. If you have overlaps in a vinyl covering that refuse to stay down, buy some of the special paste made for vinyl-to-vinyl adhesion. An application of this special paste will do the job.

3. Just when you think you did the world's smoothest papering job, you see some bubbles! Do not despair. Merely slit them twice to form an "X" across the center of the blister. Then peel back the tips of the slit and squirt paste into the blister. The tips may overlap a little, but such overlapping is seldom noticeable. If you notice the blister shortly after you finish papering—but after the paste has dried—the thick blob under the blister may still be wet paste. Try sticking a pin in the blister and then forcing the paste out. If that trick does not do the job, slit and repaste.

4. Patching a torn section of wallpaper is easy to do—provided you saved the scraps from the original papering job. Select a scrap section that matches the pattern, and tear the patch in an irregular shape so that the edge can be feathered back under the patch. Such a patch blends in much better than if it were cut evenly.

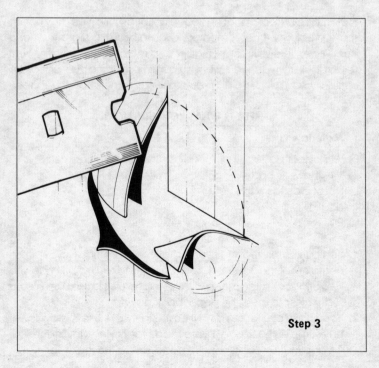

Step 3

Interior Painting

38

DO YOU HAVE interior walls that need repainting? Few do-it-yourself projects can make such a dramatic improvement in the appearance of your home and few can save you so much money over having the job done professionally. Painting can be fun, and it is easy to do well if you follow the rules. Even if you have never painted before, you can produce professional results by just following some simple directions.

Always buy top quality paint. In most cases, latex paint is your best bet. It goes on easily, dries fast, and cleans up with soap and water. After the paint dries fully, you can wash the surfaces without fear of damaging the appearance of your walls and ceilings.

The first key to a good paint job is preparation. Here are the basic steps for interior wall and ceiling preparation.

HERE IS WHAT YOU WILL NEED

Materials	Tools
☐ Spackling paste	☐ Hammer
☐ Wall cleaner	☐ Putty knife
☐ Liquid deglosser	☐ Paint scraper
☐ Drop cloths or newspapers	☐ Screwdriver
☐ Masking tape or shirtboard	☐ Measuring tape
☐ Plastic bags	☐ Mixing stick
☐ Latex interior paint	☐ Roller with extension handle
☐ Latex enamel	☐ Roller tray
☐ Primer	☐ Paintbrushes
☐ Rags	

1. Inspect walls and ceilings for any protruding nails. If you find any, drive them back in and cover them with spackling paste.
2. Patch any cracks or holes.
3. Scrape away any loose or flaking paint.
4. Clean the wall and ceiling surfaces. If they are merely dusty, brushing may be all that you need to do. If there are grease spots or other dirt, however, wash your walls and ceilings.

5. Degloss any shiny surface. You can buy liquid deglossing prepa-
rations at a paint store.
6. Move all furniture, pictures, drapes, rugs, and plants out of the
room if possible. Protect everything that must stay in the room
with drop cloths or newspapers.
7. Mask all trim that is adjacent to wall areas that you will paint.
8. Remove wall outlet plates and switch plates.
9. Loosen light fixtures and let them hang down. Then wrap the
fixtures in plastic bags.

With the preparation completed, you are ready to start painting.
Do the ceilings first, walls next, and woodwork last. Use a roller
with an extension handle for painting ceilings, and follow this
procedure.

1. Mix the paint thoroughly.
2. Use a brush to paint a border along the edge of the ceiling. This
technique is called *cutting in.*

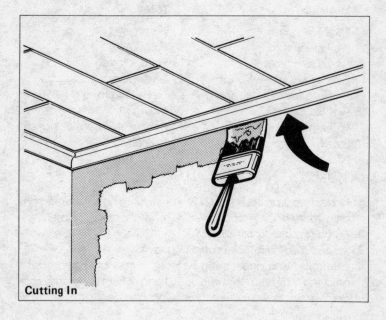

Cutting In

3. Dampen the roller slightly with the appropriate thinner.
4. Fill the roller tray with paint, load the roller, and roll it across the tray grid to remove excess paint.
5. Start painting with the roller right next to the cut-in strip. Use slow steady strokes, working back and forth over the width of the ceiling. Fast strokes spin the roller and can sling paint. Use cross strokes to smooth the paint on the ceiling.

Step 6

6. Keep working in strips across, always working against the wet edge of previously painted strips. If you allow a strip of paint to dry, you may leave streaks when you paint over it. Therefore, be sure to paint the entire ceiling without stopping.

For wall painting, follow the same procedure just described for painting ceilings.

1. Cut in along corners and around doors and windows.
2. Start in the left-hand corner if you are right handed. Begin at the top and work up and down all the way, moving the roller across as you finish each strip. Again, use cross strokes to smooth; always

work against the wet edge; and avoid having to stop in the middle of a wall.

3. Roll horizontally to paint the narrow strips over doors and windows.
4. If you did not mask the woodwork with tape, use a shirtboard as a moving masker. Should you happen to get some wall paint on the trim, use a rag to wipe it off as you go.

When you finish all the wall, you are ready to go to work on the woodwork. You should use an enamel on the trim, and it should have some gloss to it. A glossy enamel is easier to clean than a flat paint.

1. Clean all trim surfaces and remove the gloss by sanding or by applying a surface preparation chemical available at the paint store. These chemicals degloss and also leave a tacky surface that makes the new paint adhere better. Be sure to follow the directions on the label.
2. Mix the enamel paint thoroughly.
3. Although you can use rollers or foam paint pads to paint large

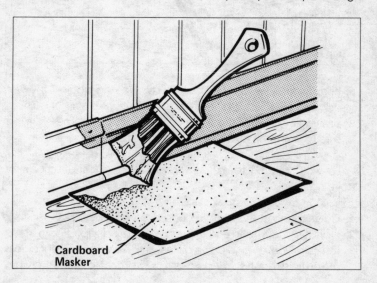

Cardboard Masker

flat areas, appropriately sized brushes are better for painting most woodwork.

4. Start with the baseboards and use a moving masker as you paint.
5. Do the windows next, but be sure to mask the panes of glass and to open the sash about three or four inches before you start painting. Then, after you paint but before the paint starts to set, move the sash up or down to prevent the window from sticking.
6. Do the doors and door frames last. Remove all hardware before painting the doors, and make sure that the enamel is dry before reinstalling the hardware.

Exterior Painting

39

THE SAME TRICKS of the trade for interior painting apply to exterior painting as well. Preparation is again a big part of a successful paint job. Here are the steps to follow to prepare exterior walls.

HERE IS WHAT YOU WILL NEED

Materials	Tools
☐ Caulk	☐ Caulking gun
☐ Sandpaper	☐ Paint scraper or wire brush
☐ Primer	☐ Hammer
☐ Tarpulin or plastic sheets	☐ Garden hose
☐ Latex or oil-based exterior paint	☐ Ladder or scaffolding
	☐ Mixing stick
	☐ Nailset
	☐ Paintbrushes

1. Caulk around all doors and windows and any other joints that might let in moisture or air.
2. Repair or replace any damaged wood or other exterior siding material.

3. Remove all loose paint with either a scraper or a wire brush. Feather any chipped edges by sanding away the sharp edges of the remaining paint.
4. Reset any loose nails.
5. Prime all bare spots with a primer suggested for use with the paint you have selected. Latex exterior paint offers the same ease of application and cleaning as latex interior paint, and—when used properly—it provides long lasting coverage. Nevertheless, some people still prefer oil-based paint for exterior use.
6. Be sure to remove any mildew on exterior surfaces.
7. Make sure that all surfaces you intend to paint are clean. Hose off any loose dirt.
8. Wait until the surfaces are dry before starting to paint.
9. Cover walks, drives, patios, and shrubs with tarp. Plastic suit bags from the dry cleaners are very handy for wrapping shrubbery.

You will get the best results if you paint the outside of your house when the temperature is mild, the humidity is low to moderate, and when no rain is forecast. Naturally, you must take the proper safety precautions. If you are going to rely on a ladder, make sure that it is sturdy and tall enough for you to reach all areas without stretching. Although buying scaffolding for a job you do only once every few years makes no sense, renting scaffolding does. Most rental companies can provide the scaffolding you need at very reasonable rates.

With all the preparation completed, you are ready to start painting your house. Follow these simple steps for professional results.

1. Mix the paint well.
2. Try not to paint in the hot sun.
3. Start at the top, completing all broad main areas first. Work in a band across the width, painting a swath of about three to four feet wide, and continue painting such bands all the way down.
4. When you finish the main part of the house, go back and paint the trim. Pad the ends of a straight ladder that must rest against the newly painted areas in order not to mar the new paint job.
5. Wait to apply a second coat until the first one is fully dry.

Painting Doors, Windows, and Shutters

40

WHEN IT COMES to putting a coat of paint on doors or windows, you will get much better results if you follow the prescribed sequence. You may have been lucky and had good results before without even knowing that there was such a sequence, but by following these guidelines you can be certain that your doors and windows will come out looking professionally painted.

First, consider painting a paneled door. You should arrange to have the time to finish the door completely without stopping.

HERE IS WHAT YOU WILL NEED

Materials	Tools
☐ Latex paint	☐ Paintbrushes
☐ Masking tape	

1. Start with the inset panels at the top, painting all the panels and molding around them.
2. Next, paint across the top rail.
3. Work on down to cover other horizontal rails.
4. Finish the door by painting the side rails.
5. If both sides of the door need painting, follow the same sequence before painting the edges.
6. Now, paint the top edge, followed by the hinge and latch edges.

Here is the step-by-step procedure for painting double-hung windows. Begin by masking the glass.

1. Raise the bottom sash more than half way up, and then lower the upper sash until the bottom rail of the upper sash is several inches below the top rail of the lower sash.
2. Paint the lower rail of the upper sash and on up the sides (stiles) as far as you can go.

117

3. Next, paint the outside and inside channels as far as you can go above the lower sash.

4. Paint across the head jamb.

5. Now lower both windows, and paint the outside and then inside channels on both sides.

6. Raise both windows and paint the remainder of the two channels.

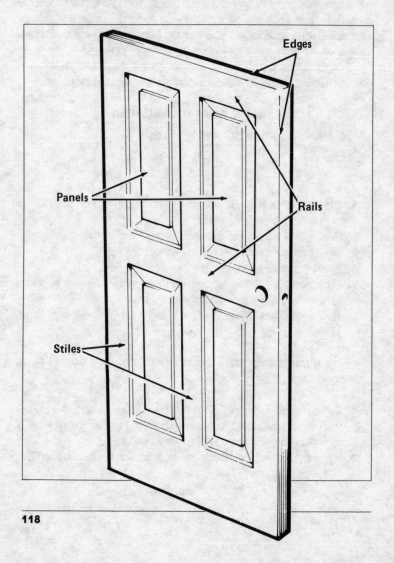

7. Lower the bottom sash and finish the stiles and top rail of the upper sash.

8. Raise the lower sash a few inches and paint it.

9. Be sure to move both the upper and lower sash before the paint can dry, sealing the sash and causing them to stick.

10. Remove the masking tape.

Shutters seldom require much of a sequence, but they usually turn out much better if you remove them from the wall before painting.

1. Examine the shutters to see how they are attached. Decorative shutters are often nailed in place (even to brick walls).

2. Do whatever you must to remove the shutters, and then lay them on a flat surface.

3. Use a narrow brush to paint the louvers first, the frame second, and the edges last.

Paint double-hung windows in the sequence shown for access to all surfaces.

41 Paintbrush Care

ALMOST EVERY painting expert recommends buying only top quality brushes. You would be wise to follow the experts' advice. If you fail to take proper care of your brushes, though, even the best ones might not last beyond the first paint job. On the other hand, a good paintbrush can give you years of service when you take proper care of it. Here are some rules to follow to extend the life of your brushes.

HERE IS WHAT YOU WILL NEED

Materials	Tools
☐ Soap or detergent	☐ Comb
☐ Paint thinner or turpentine	☐ Wire brush or putty knife
☐ Wood alcohol	
☐ Lacquer thinner	
☐ Aluminum foil	
☐ Linseed oil	
☐ Brush cleaner	

1. Never use your brush to stir paint. To do so could cause it to become floppy. Instead, use wooden mixing paddles available free at the paint store.
2. Never dip your brush into the paint bucket more than half way up the bristles. You should try to prevent paint from getting into the heel.
3. Never paint with the side of your brush. That causes curling.
4. To remove excess paint, tap the brush against the inside of the can instead of drawing the brush across the edge of the can. The latter method can cause the bristles to separate into clumps.
5. Never leave the brush in the bucket. Its own weight will bend the bristles against the bottom of the can and cause them to curl.
6. If you stop painting for a short period of time while applying a latex paint, wrap the brush in a damp paper towel or insert it in a plastic sandwich bag. Latex paint dries quickly, and partially

dried paint in a brush can stiffen the bristles.

7. Pick the right brush for the job. For example, use only nylon brushes for latex paint. No brush is capable of doing all your painting, and forcing a brush to do things it is not shaped or sized to do will damage the brush.

The best way to get the most mileage out of a brush is to clean it immediately after each use. Here are the basics of brush cleaning.

1. The solution in which you clean your brush can make a big difference. For latex paints, use soap or detergent and warm water; avoid putting nylon brushes in solvents. For oil-based paints, use paint thinner or turpentine. For shellac, use wood alcohol. For lacquer, use lacquer thinner. For varnish, use paint thinner or turpentine.

2. Let the brush soak for a few minutes to saturate the bristles completely. Make sure to use enough cleaner to cover all of the bristles. Suspend the brush in such a way that the bristles do not rest on the bottom of the container.

3. Work the brush against the side of the container for several minutes to get the paint out.

4. Squeeze the bristles with your hands. Start at the heel of the brush and work to the tip.

5. Work the brush against a section of newspaper to remove excess

Support Rod

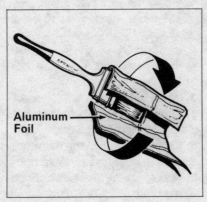

Aluminum Foil

solvent and to check whether all the paint is gone. If there is still some paint present, repeat the cleaning process.

6. With latex paint, you can just rinse the brush out by holding it under a faucet.

7. When the brush is clean, shake out the excess solvent or water and comb out the bristles.

8. Wash solvent-cleaned brushes in warm soapy water, and comb them again to separate the inner bristles and to allow the brushes to dry straight.

Even a clean brush must be stored correctly or it will go bad before you need to use it again. Here are some storage hints.

1. Always let brushes dry by suspending them with the bristles down.

2. Wrap natural bristle brushes in aluminum foil after they have dried. Wrap carefully to hold the brush in its proper shape during storage, and pour in a little linseed oil before crimping the foil around the handle.

If you neglected your brushes and now they are hard with caked paint, here are some steps you can take to restore them to usefulness.

1. Go to the paint store and buy a commercial brush cleaner. Some are liquid, while others are dry and must be mixed with water.

2. Let the brush soak in the cleaner. If there is dried paint up under the metal band, make sure that the brush gets into the cleaner that deep.

3. When the cleaner has softened the paint sufficiently, use a wire brush or putty knife to scrape the residue away. Work from the metal band downward.

4. Rinse the brush in the cleaner. If you still can see caked paint, soak the brush some more and repeat the cleaning steps.

5. Now follow all the steps as if you had just finished painting with the brush.

You will not be able to reclaim all your old brushes caked with paint, but it is worth a try because brush cleaner costs much less than new brushes. If you treat your paintbrushes properly from the start, of course, you need never go through this process again.

The Clogged Drain   42

IT IS NOT surprising that home drain lines get clogged up. All kinds of things seem to go down the sink: grease, coffee grounds, leftover salad, table scraps, and even cigarette butts. Then one day, the kitchen sink backs up and you have a repair on your hands.

You should be able to clear the clogged drain with a plunger. Since many clogs are close at hand, the plunger can usually build up enough force and direct it against the clog to solve the problem. There are aerosol drain openers on the market that do the same thing, but they are no more effective than the plunger and are considerably more expensive. Just make sure that the rubber cup is big enough to cover the opening in the sink, and then follow these directions.

HERE IS WHAT YOU WILL NEED

Materials	Tools
☐ Aerosol drain opener	☐ Plunger
☐ Chemical drain cleaner	☐ Plumber's snake (auger)
☐ Pipe joint compound or petroleum jelly	☐ Adjustable wrench or pliers

1. Cover any other openings to the drain pipe such as the other side of a double sink or an overflow drain.
2. Remove the stopper and/or strainer.
3. Brush aside the garbage around the drain opening.
4. Have at least an inch of water standing in the sink.
5. Place the cup of the plunger over the drain opening.

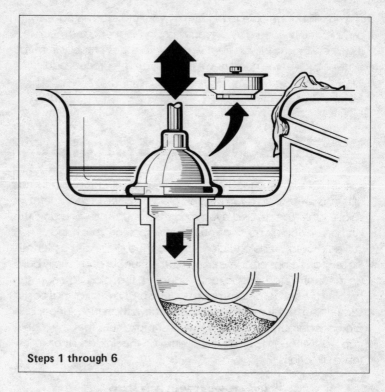

Steps 1 through 6

6. Position the plunger firmly in place over the drain, and start an up-and-down motion to force the water back and forth in the pipe. The down stroke pushes the water down, and the up stroke creates a vacuum that pulls it back. Once you build up a rhythm, you will be able to feel the force of the water going back and forth.
7. After about 15 to 20 strokes, lift the plunger up.
8. If the water does not swirl out of the sink and down the drain, try the plunger procedure at least once again.

The next thing most people try on a clogged drain is a chemical drain cleaner. These chemicals are caustic and they can be dangerous. If they fail to do the job, they remain in your pipes, and you must be very careful not to splash this water on you or on anything that would be damaged.

The next best step to take after using the plunger is to drive a plumber's snake or auger into the drain pipe. The tool is so flexible that it can make its way around all the curves inside a drain pipe until it reaches the clog. Here is how to use the plumber's snake.

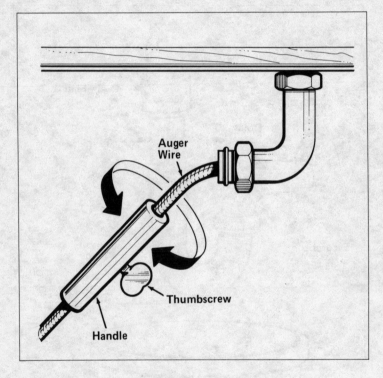

1. Remove the stopper and/or strainer in the sink.
2. Feed the snake into the drain.
3. When it hits a turn, slide the handle up to within a few inches of the opening, tighten it, and start turning the snake until it negotiates the turn.
4. Loosen the handle and slide it back out of the way.
5. Keep feeding the snake in until it hits either another turn or the

clog. Set the handle once more.
6. When you finally do hit the clog, work the snake back and forth while at the same time turning the handle.
7. When you feel the clog break loose, pull the snake back and forth a few more times, and then remove it from the drain pipe.
8. Flush the line with hot water.

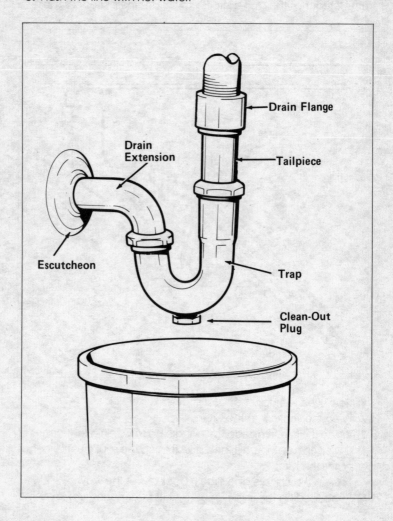

If you cannot get the snake down the sink drain, you can remove the trap under the sink and insert the snake there. The trap is that U-shaped pipe under every sink or basin. It is a good idea in general to know how to remove the trap because rings and contact lenses often go down the drain and get caught in the trap. Here is how to remove the trap.

1. Place a bucket under the trap to catch all the water in the sink and in the trap.
2. If you see a plug in the bottom of the trap, turn it counterclockwise with an adjustable wrench to remove the slip nuts holding the trap to the sink and drain pipe. You will need either large pliers or a large adjustable wrench to turn the nuts counterclockwise. Make sure that you do not lose the washers under the nuts.
3. Check to see if the clog is in the trap itself. If so, clean it out with a piece of wire or with the plumber's snake.
4. If the clog is not in the trap, run the snake in at the cleanout plug or into the pipe leading into the wall, following the same procedures as above.
5. When replacing the trap or plug, smear some pipe joint compound (available at the hardware store) or some petroleum jelly on the threads.
6. After the pipe is securely in place, run the water for a few minutes to make sure that you have the trap back together properly so that it will not leak.

Unclogging a Toilet 43

FOR SOME REASON, children have a tendency to put things in the toilet that clog up the pipes. Adults can be guilty as well, placing items on the tank lid that accidentally get knocked into the bowl. A plunger will usually clear the clog. You should be aware, though, that there is a plunger made especially for toilets. It has a special tapered lip that fits down snugly into the bowl. If you have frequent toilet clog troubles in your home, invest in a toilet plunger and then follow these steps.

HERE IS WHAT YOU WILL NEED

Materials	Tools
☐ Wire coat hanger	☐ Plunger
	☐ Closet snake (auger)

1. Make sure that there is enough water in the bowl to cover the plunger, and then place the plunger over the outlet in the bottom. Keep in mind that you must allow room for the extra water the plunger will bring back into the bowl.
2. Push down on the plunger's handle, and start a steady up-and-down motion.

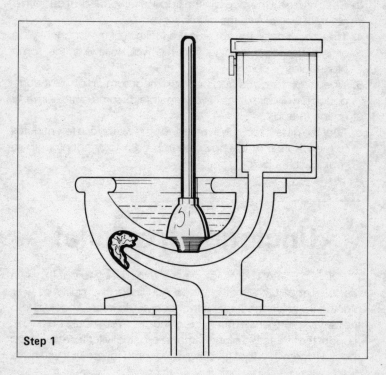

Step 1

3. When you can feel that the force created by the plunger has the water rocking back and forth, lift the plunger out and check to see if any matter has been dislodged. If you unclog the drain, some of the water will probably rush out. If you dislodge a big wad of paper, use a wire coat hanger to break it up.

4. Pour some water from another source into the bowl; do not trip the handle to flush the toilet. Flushing the toilet while the clog is still present will produce an overflow, while pouring in some water from another source will tell you whether your work with the plunger did the job.

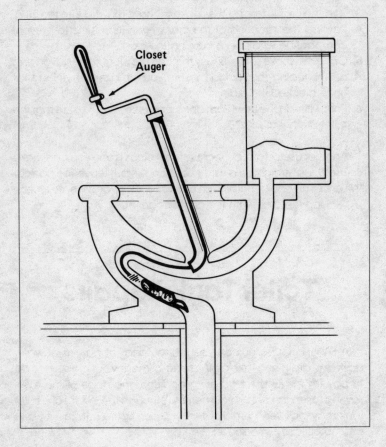

Closet Auger

Stubborn clogs often require the use of a closet snake, a shorter version of the plumber's snake. Sometimes referred to as a *closet auger*, the closet snake has a crank at one end with a hollow metal tube housing the snake itself. You do not need a long snake for toilets, since the blockage cannot be very far away. Just be careful not to bang the auger against the bowl; it could break the porcelain. Here is what to do with the closet auger.

1. Insert the snake into the outflow opening.
2. Push it in until it hits the clog.
3. Turn the crank, forcing the snake to move forward into the clog.
4. Reverse the direction of the crank every few turns to prevent compacting whatever is causing the clog.
5. Once the snake works its way through the clog, keep advancing and reversing the tool to be sure you remove everything that once blocked the drain.
6. Pour water in the bowl from another source to make sure that the toilet drain is clear.

Another useful tool for clearing toilet clogs is one you can make yourself. Just straighten a wire coat hanger, but leave the hook at the end. You can generally fish out paper clogs and whatever else is blocking the drain with the coat hanger hook.

44   Toilet Tank Repairs

A FAULTY TOILET tank can send thousands of gallons of water down the drain and take a great deal of money out of your pocket to pay for the wasted water. In addition, the noise of the ever-flowing toilet can get on your nerves. Although the insides of a toilet tank may look very complicated, you can figure out how it works with no difficulty whatsoever.

HERE IS WHAT YOU WILL NEED

Materials	Tools
☐ Replacement guide wires or trip lever	☐ Knife
☐ Replacement tank ball	
☐ Wet-dry emery paper or steel wool	
☐ Replacement washers for valve of ball cock assembly	

How the toilet works:

1. You push the handle to flush.
2. The handle raises the trip lever inside the tank.
3. Since the trip lever is attached to the lift wires, they go up too.
4. The lift wires raise the tank ball from where it rests in an outflow hole, allowing water in the tank to run out into the bowl and clean it.
5. Meanwhile, the float ball—which had been floating on the top of the water in the tank—drops as the water rushes out.
6. The float arm moves down with the float ball, opening the valve, which lets new water flow into the tank.
7. The tank ball falls back in place in the overflow hole, causing the new water to fill the tank.
8. As the water rises in the tank, it picks up the float ball and moves the float arm back up until the valve closes and no more water can enter.

Now that you know how the tank works, you can follow the procedure for fixing a continually running toilet.

1. Remove the tank lid very carefully, and place it out of the way where it cannot fall or be stepped upon.
2. Reach in and lift up on the float arm. If the water stops running, you know the problem is that the arm does not rise far enough to shut off the valve. Merely bend the float arm down slightly to correct the situation.

3. If the float arm is not the problem, look to see whether the tank ball is properly seated. If you cannot tell by looking, turn off the water supply under the tank. A toilet that continues to run is one in which water is seeping out around the outflow opening. Make sure that the guide is in place so that the wires are directly above the opening. Rotate the guide until the tank ball falls straight down into the outflow hole. If you see any bent wires or a trip lever that is not exactly where it should be, bend the parts back in

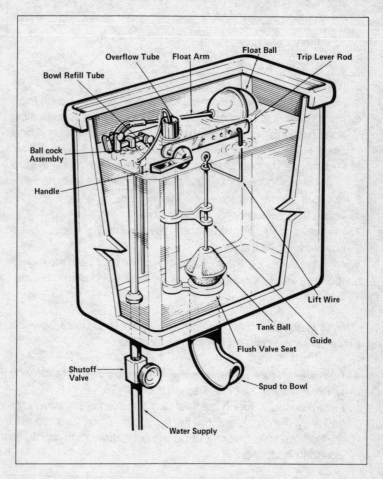

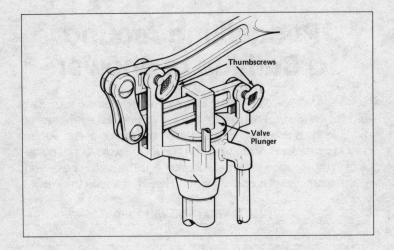

shape or install new ones. Occasionally the tank ball wears out, but it is easy to replace too. If all the parts seem to be in good shape, inspect the valve seat for corrosion on its lip. Such corrosion may be preventing the tank ball from sealing the opening. You can remove the residue with wet-dry emery paper, steel wool, or a knife.

4. If the toilet continues to run, then something is probably wrong with the valve in the ball cock assembly. This valve has one or more washers (often including a split leather washer) that can be replaced. To get at the washers, remove the two thumbscrews and lift the valve out. Replace any and all faulty washers.

Here are some other basic repairs for toilet tanks.

1. If the toilet makes a screaming noise as it fills, but works properly otherwise, replace the washers in the ball cock assembly valve.

2. If the flush is inadequate, make certain that the level of water in the tank is sufficient; it should be about ½ inch below the top of the overflow tube. If the water level is too low, bend the float arm up slightly. An inadequate flush might also result from the tank ball not going up far enough. Raise the guide to give the tank ball more room.

45

Recaulking Around a Bathtub or Shower

WHEN YOUR CAULKING breaks loose, the crack that forms around the tub may not look terrible, but you should fix it immediately. As long as there is a gap between the tub and wall, you are letting water seep in. The seepage can rot the walls, cause mildew with its musty odors to form inside, damage the ceiling below, and even loosen the tiles above the tub. Here is how to fix the crack.

HERE IS WHAT YOU WILL NEED

Materials	Tools
☐ Bathtub caulking	☐ Putty knife
☐ Cleaning solvent	☐ Razor blade (with safety
☐ Rags	edge)

1. Purchase a tube of the caulk made especially for bathtubs; it differs from the regular caulk. Some manufacturers of tub caulk offer their product in colors, allowing you to match the color of the tub.

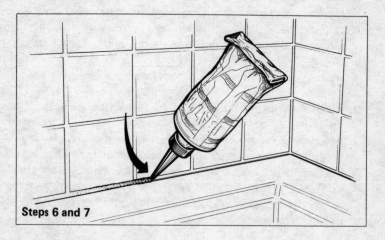

Steps 6 and 7

2. Remove all of the old caulk. Use a putty knife, and be careful not to chip the surface of the tub or the edges of the bottom row of tiles.
3. Use a solvent to clean away any soap residue.
4. Rinse away the solvent with water.
5. Make sure that the surface is completely dry by wrapping a cloth around the putty knife blade and running it through the seam.
6. Cut the nozzle of the tub caulk tube at an angle and at a point where the size bead that comes out will be slightly wider than the cavity around the tub.
7. Squeeze the caulk in one continuous bead all around the tub.
8. Wrap a rag around your index finger, dip your finger into a glass of water, and then press the caulk into the cavity. Keep dipping as you go whenever the rag loses its moisture. Smooth the caulk as you push it in.

Done correctly, this should last for a long time. Quality caulk has elasticity, allowing it to stretch and compress as the weight in the tub changes.

Plumbing Pipe Leaks   46

WHEN A PIPE bursts, it can do tremendous damage to your home. But there are measures you can take to prevent major destruction. If you act quickly and follow these steps, you can turn a potential disaster into an easy do-it-yourself repair job.

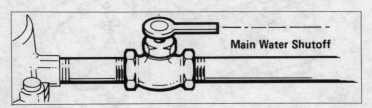

Main Water Shutoff

HERE IS WHAT YOU WILL NEED

Materials	Tools
☐ Pipe patching kit (clamps, rubber pad, and bolts) or inner tube scrap and worm gear hose clamp	☐ Pipe wrench
	☐ Propane torch
	☐ Hacksaw
☐ Waterproof tape	
☐ Epoxy metal	
☐ Pipe joint compound	
☐ Solder	
☐ New pipe	
☐ Union fitting	
☐ Solvent weld compound	

1. Shut off the water. If there is a cutoff for just that section of pipe, shut it off. If not, go to the main water cutoff for your home and turn it off.

2. Locate and examine the leaky section.

3. If the leak is in the middle of a length of galvanized pipe, there are several ways to clamp a patch over the hole. You can buy a kit at the hardware store that includes a pair of clamps, a rubber pad, and bolts. Or you can apply the same sort of patch with a

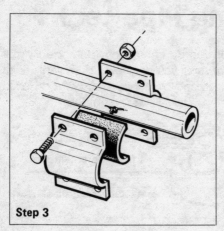

Step 3

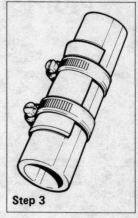

Step 3

scrap of inner tube and a worm gear hose clamp.

4. For a temporary repair of a small leak, you can wrap waterproof tape around any type of pipe. The tape should cover several inches to either side of the hole.

5. You can apply epoxy metal to any metal pipe. Be sure to allow the pipe to dry completely, and then follow the directions for curing time.

6. Leaks around pipe joints are more common than burst pipes. Galvanized pipe joints are threaded, and sometimes they just need to be tightened. If tightening fails to stop the leak, loosen the fitting, apply pipe joint compound, and retighten. A compression fitting that leaks probably just needs a slight tightening; but joints in copper tubing that leak must be removed, all the old solder cleaned away, the tubing dried completely, and then the joint resoldered.

7. A bad section of pipe should be replaced rather than patched. Cut out the bad part, and replace it with two shorter pipe sections joined by a fitting—called a union—that goes in the middle.

8. If the leak is in plastic pipe, try to use solvent weld compound to seal the leak. If the compound does not do the job, replace the bad section of pipe.

Repairing a Dripping Faucet 47

AMONG THE MORE harmless of household problems is the dripping faucet. Most people reason that a drip just amounts to a few drops of wasted water, so why worry? Yet, if you stop to add up how much water is wasted in a year, the cost can mount up. If you call for a plumber to fix it, of course, he will charge you, but you can repair a dripping faucet in a few minutes, and the parts cost will be minimal. You will find it an easy repair if you follow these steps.

HERE IS WHAT YOU WILL NEED

Materials	Tools
☐ Masking tape	☐ Adjustable wrench
☐ Replacement washer	☐ Screwdriver
☐ Replacement seat	☐ Reseating tool or valve seat grinder
☐ Petroleum jelly	
☐ Replacement packing	
☐ Repair kit for single-handle faucet	

1. Shut off the water at the cutoff below the sink or at the main cutoff where the water supply pipe enters your home.

2. Remove the packing nut with an adjustable wrench. You may first have to flip up a button, remove the screw under it, and slip the handle off to expose the packing nut. In some cases, you will find a setscrew holding the handle; remove it and the handle to get at the packing nut. If the packing nut is highly visible or made of chrome, protect it from the wrench by wrapping it with masking tape.

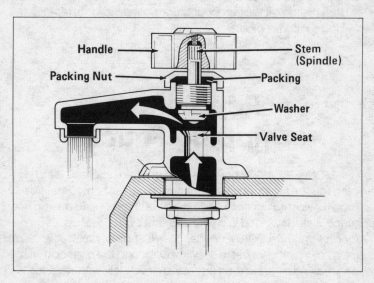

3. With the packing nut off, turn the spindle out.

4. At the bottom of the spindle you will see the washer held in place by a brass screw.

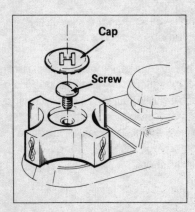
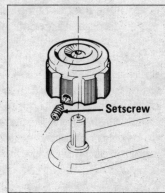

5. Remove the brass screw, and replace the washer with a new one of the same size. Reinstall the brass screw.

6. Inspect the seat down in the faucet. If it is scarred or corroded, either clean and reface it with an inexpensive reseating tool or replace the seat itself. The reseating tool or valve seat grinder has cutting teeth. Insert the tool in the faucet and install the packing nut over it; then turn the handle to screw the tool down against the seat, causing the cutting teeth to grind the seat smooth. Make sure that the seat is smooth and shiny after using the tool.

7. Coat the threads of the spindle with petroleum jelly.

8. Reassemble the faucet, and turn the water back on.

If your faucet leaks around the handle only when the water is turned on, you need to replace the packing. Here is how to do that simple repair procedure.

1. Remove the spindle as in Steps 1, 2, and 3 above.

2. If you have not already removed the handle to get to the packing nut, remove the handle now.

3. Slide the packing nut up off the spindle.

4. The blob under the packing nut is the packing. It may be a solid piece, or it may be a string of black graphite material that is self-forming. Replace the old packing with new packing of the same type.

5. Coat the threads of the spindle with petroleum jelly.

6. Reassemble the faucet and turn the water back on.

Another type of faucet that is very popular in newer homes is the single-handle version. One lever controls both the hot and cold water. Every maker of such faucets markets a repair kit containing all the parts that you might have to replace. The kit also offers detailed instructions on how to work with the faucet. All you have to do is find a company that carries your brand of faucet, buy the repair kit, and then follow the instructions.

48 Taking Care of a Hot Water Heater

POSSIBLY THE sturdiest appliance you will ever own is your hot water heater. Most new units carry a guarantee on all parts, with an even longer guarantee (often up to 10 years) on the tank. Whether you have a gas, electric, or oil-heated unit, usually the only maintenance you need to do is drain the tank periodically to prevent sediment from building up in the tank. In many areas you may need to drain monthly, depending on the hardness of the water and on the type of chemicals added. Here is how to drain your hot water heater.

HERE IS WHAT YOU WILL NEED

Materials	Tools
☐ None	☐ Garden hose
	☐ Bucket or small container

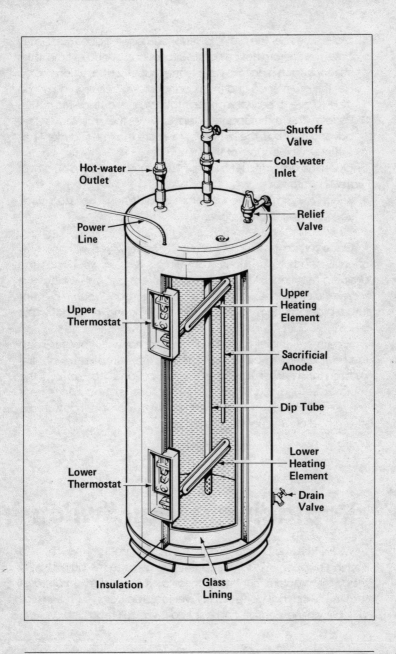

1. Make sure that the drain valve turns easily. If it does not, it may have frozen from not being used for a long period of time. If it is frozen, attach a garden hose to the faucet so that when you do get the drain open and then cannot close it readily, you will be able to direct the water either into a drain or outside the house.

2. Perform this maintenance step early in the morning before anyone has used the hot water to insure that the sediment has settled to the bottom of the tank.

3. Open the drain and let a few pints of water flow into a bucket or small container.

4. Keep draining until the water runs clear. When it does run clear, your draining chore is done.

Once you do this task several months in a row, you will know how often it needs to be done. Sometimes, twice a year is all the draining required. By keeping the sediment out, you will have a more efficient and less noisy hot water system, and you will prevent future problems from developing in the tank and in the hot water pipes.

For a more efficient and longer lasting hot water heater, keep the heat control at a moderate setting. The temperature control knob on most heaters has "warm," "normal," and "hot" settings. The "normal" setting, usually about 140 degrees, is about all the heat you need. If you set the water heater control too high, it can create steam and cause knocking noises in the pipes.

49 Replacing a Wall Switch

WHEN YOU WALK into a dark room, flip the light switch, and nothing happens, your first impulse is to change the bulb. Usually that is the problem, but one of these days you just might discover that the switch has gone bad. Never fear, replacing a broken wall switch is an inexpensive and easy do-it-yourself repair job.

If the switch is the only one that controls the fixture, it is called a single-pole switch. If there are two switches that control the same light, then it is called a three-way switch. Here is how to replace a single-pole switch.

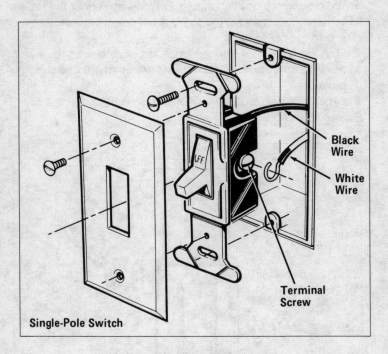

Black Wire

White Wire

Terminal Screw

Single-Pole Switch

HERE IS WHAT YOU WILL NEED

Materials	Tools
☐ Replacement single-pole or three-way switch	☐ Screwdriver

1. **Cut off the power to the switch;** unscrew the appropriate fuse or trip the appropriate circuit breaker switch.
2. Remove the cover plate by turning the screws on its face counterclockwise.
3. Remove the two screws holding the switch to the junction box.

4. Grasp the switch and pull it out from the box. It should come out several inches.

5. Remove the two wires to the switch by turning the screws counterclockwise.

6. The new switch has two screws. Put the wires under the screws with the curls going in the same direction—clockwise. Turn the screws to tighten them.

7. Push the wires back into the junction box, and press the switch back against the box. Reinstall the screws that hold the switch in place.

8. Replace the cover plate with its face screws.

9. Restore the power.

Three-Way Switch

If you have a three-way switch, very little more is involved. The difference is that a three-way switch has an extra wire, usually a red one. All of the same safety precautions apply to changing such a switch. All you do differently is make a note of where each wire is attached to the old switch, and then attach the wires the same way to the new three-way switch.

Replacing a Lamp Socket 50

DO YOU HAVE a lamp that flickers, or one that just will not work no matter what you do? The problem could be a defective bulb, plug, wiring, or socket. If you find that the socket is the culprit, you can repair it easily and safely. Socket repairs are made without any electrical current flowing to the lamp. It makes no difference whether your lamp has a pull chain, a push-button switch, or no switch at all; all conventional sockets are installed in the same manner. Even three-way sockets hook up the same way.

HERE IS WHAT YOU WILL NEED

Materials	Tools
☐ Replacement socket	☐ Screwdriver
	☐ Wire cutters
	☐ Insulation stripper or knife

1. **Unplug the lamp.**
2. Remove the bulb.
3. Remove the old socket from its base or cap. Usually all you have to do is press on the brass outer shell with your thumb and forefinger, but stubborn sockets may require that you pry them out with a screwdriver.
4. Slide off the cardboard insulating sleeve.
5. Loosen the screws that hold the two wires to the socket.
6. Check the wires. The tiny strands must be twisted to form a

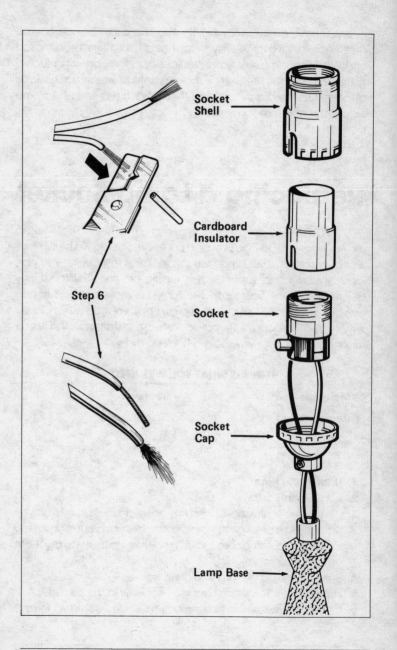

Socket Shell

Cardboard Insulator

Step 6

Socket

Socket Cap

Lamp Base

single unit with no stray strands. If the ends are in disarray, snip them off and strip the insulation back to expose about ¾ inch of bare strands. Twist the strands into one neat wire.

7. Curl the wire ends in a clockwise direction to fit around the screws of the new socket.

8. Tighten the screws.

9. Replace the insulating sleeve and outer shell back over the socket.

10. Snap the entire unit back into the lamp base, and check to make sure that it is in good and tight.

11. Install the bulb and plug in the lamp.

Many ceiling and wall fixtures possess the same type of sockets as found on standard table lamps. The installation is just about the same, but since you cannot unplug a wall or ceiling fixture, you must unscrew the fuse or trip the circuit breaker to make certain that no current goes to the fixture while you are working on it.

Fixing a Doorbell 51

IT IS AMAZING how many people shy away from trying to fix a faulty doorbell, considering what a simple hookup is involved. There are only four components to check, and the first one you look at—the push button—is usually the problem. Fortunately, the button is also the easiest component to fix. The other components are the bell or chime unit, the transformer, and the wiring.

You should be aware of how much electric current you will be facing. A doorbell runs on very low voltage. A single button unit may operate on only 12 volts, while a unit with separate buttons at the front and back may involve from 16 to 24 volts. Most doorbell repair experts will tell you that these voltages are too low for you to bother cutting the power to the circuit, but even though none of these voltages can harm you, 24 volts is enough to make you feel the shock. Therefore, try to avoid touching the wires while troubleshooting, and then cut the power while doing the repairs.

HERE IS WHAT YOU WILL NEED

Materials	Tools
☐ Sandpaper	☐ Screwdriver
☐ Replacement button	☐ Knife
☐ Cleaning solvent	☐ 12-volt test light
☐ Replacement bell unit	☐ Electrical testing light
☐ Replacement transformer	
☐ Replacement wiring	

1. First, check the button. Buttons wear out and go bad before any of the other components in most cases. To check the push button, remove its faceplate.
2. Disconnect the wires to the button unit.
3. Touch the two wires together. If the bell rings, you know that everything else is in good shape. The trouble is in the button itself.
4. Scrape the ends of the wires and sand the contact points on the button to get rid of any corrosion.
5. Hook up the wires again and try the button. If it still fails to work, purchase a new button.
6. On the other hand, if the bell failed to ring when you touched the wires together, you know that the problem lies elsewhere. The next part to check is the buzzer or chime unit. Check the connec-

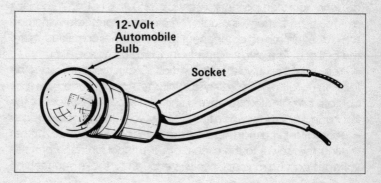

12-Volt
Automobile
Bulb

Socket

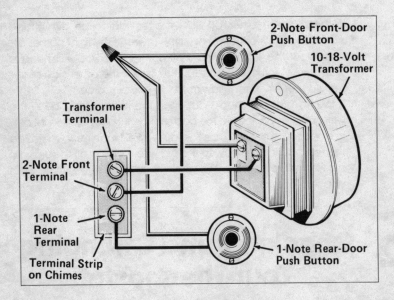

tions going into the unit to make sure that the wires are clean and that the terminals are tight. Inspect the bell clapper to make certain that it is close enough to the bell to hit it. If you have a set of chimes, clean the striker rods carefully with a solvent. After cleaning and checking the connections, disconnect the bell unit from its circuit and hook up a 12-volt test light (you can make one with a 12-volt auto bulb in a socket with two wires coming from it) to check the bell unit itself. If the light glows when you push the doorbell, you need a new bell. With a unit that has a back door button, remove only the wire marked "transformer" and one other—either the one marked "front" or "'rear''—and hook them to the light. If the doorbell button lights the bulb, you can be doubly certain that the trouble is in the bell unit.

7. If the unit checks out, meaning the light fails to go on when you push the door buttons, you must next test the transformer. Keep in mind that there are 110 volts on one side of the transformer; therefore be sure to unscrew the fuse or trip the circuit breaker before you touch the transformer.

8. With the power turned off, hook the test light to the low voltage side of the transformer. Restore the power. If the light comes on, you know the transformer is all right. If not, you will need a standard electrical testing light to check the other side of the transformer for current flow from the power source.

9. If the transformer checks out, then the trouble must be in the wiring. When you locate the bad section, inspect it to see if it can be repaired. If not, replace the faulty wire. To run new wire inside the walls, splice the new to the old wire. As you pull the old wire out from the other end, it will pull the new wire through the walls and into position.

52 Checking and Changing Your Thermostat

IF YOU HAVE a thermostat in your home that controls the heating and/or cooling of your house and is no longer calibrated properly, you can never be sure that you are heating or cooling your house to the temperature setting you desire. Here is how to check your thermostat's calibration.

HERE IS WHAT YOU WILL NEED

Materials	Tools
☐ Tape	☐ Plastic squeeze bottle
☐ Tube-type thermometer	☐ Screwdriver
☐ Padding	☐ Knife
☐ Replacement thermostat	☐ Level

1. Tape a glass tube thermometer to the wall a few inches from the thermostat. Place a small tab of padding under the thermometer to prevent it from actually touching the wall.

2. Wait about ten to fifteen minutes for the thermometer to stabilize.

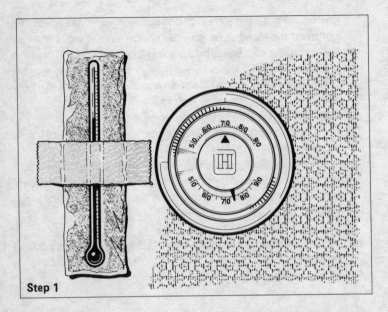

Step 1

3. Compare the reading on the glass thermometer with the needle showing the temperature on the thermostat.

If there is a variance of more than one degree, you need to do something about the thermostat. Remove the faceplate—usually held in place by a snap-in friction catch—and inspect the mechanism inside for dust particles. If there is dust inside, blow it away either with your breath or with an empty plastic squeeze bottle. Do not use a vacuum cleaner.

If there is no dust problem, you must decide whether to replace the thermostat or just learn what each setting means in terms of real temperature. If you wish to put in a new unit, here are the basic steps.

1. Make sure the power to the system is turned off.
2. With the faceplate off of the old unit, look for the mounting screws. Remove the screws to release the unit from the wall.
3. Remove the wires coming from the wall by turning the screws

on the back of the thermostat unit counterclockwise. Take care not to let the loose wires fall down between the walls.

4. Clean the exposed wires by scraping them with a knife until the wire ends shine.
5. Attach the wires to the new thermostat. Be sure that the new unit operates on the same voltage.
6. Push the excess wire back into the wall.
7. Tape up the opening to prevent cold air inside the walls from affecting the thermostat.
8. Install the mounting screws to secure the new unit to the wall. If the thermostat has a mercury tube, set the unit against a level during installation. A mercury tube thermostat is more accurate when it is level.
9. Snap the faceplate in place.
10. Make sure that the new thermostat turns the heating/cooling unit on and off when you change the temperature setting.
11. Turn your power on.

53 Replacing a Wall Outlet

VERY OFTEN, PEOPLE plug in an appliance and when nothing happens they mistakenly blame the appliance for malfunctioning when the real culprit is the wall outlet. If you have a faulty outlet, the first thing you need to determine before trying to replace it is whether you need to buy a grounded or ungrounded receptacle. You can tell the difference at a glance. The grounded outlet has a third hole for a three-pronged plug. Once you purchase the proper replacement, just follow these steps to install it.

HERE IS WHAT YOU WILL NEED

Materials	Tools
☐ Replacement grounded or ungrounded receptacle	☐ Screwdriver

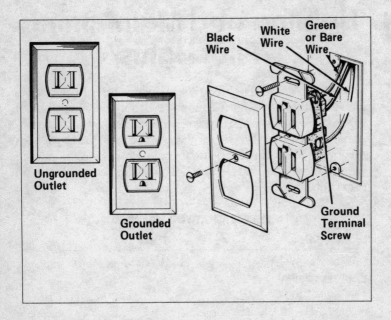

Black Wire · White Wire · Green or Bare Wire · Ungrounded Outlet · Grounded Outlet · Ground Terminal Screw

1. **Cut off the power to that circuit** by either unscrewing the fuse or tripping the circuit breaker.
2. Remove the single screw in the middle of the faceplate that holds the plate to the wall.
3. With the faceplate off, remove the two screws that hold the outlet to the junction box.
4. Pull the outlet from the box. The outlet's wires will allow it to come out several inches.
5. Before loosening the screws to remove the wires, take note of how each wire is connected. You must attach the new outlet the same way. Hook any black wires to the side with the brass screws, and white wires to the side with the silver screws. Attach the green or uninsulated wire to the green screw of a grounded outlet.
6. Push the unit back in place in the junction box and secure it with the two screws.
7. Reattach the faceplate with its screw.
8. Restore the power.

54 Lighting and Maintaining Pilot Lights

MOST APPLIANCES heated by natural gas have pilot lights to provide instant heat when you need it. No matter whether the pilot is on a hot water heater, a furnace, a range, or a clothes dryer, they all are quite similar. If you smell gas, don't hesitate to call your gas company. While the best guide for any appliance is the owner's manual, here are some general tips for lighting and maintaining pilot lights.

HERE IS WHAT YOU WILL NEED

Materials	Tools
☐ Matches	☐ Wrench
☐ Replacement thermocouple	

1. If the pilot is out, check to be sure that the gas cutoff valve and the gas cock (the "on-off" knob at the gas valve) are both at the full "on" position.
2. Unless otherwise specified, turn the gas cock to its "off" position and **wait five minutes.**
3. Turn the gas cock to the "pilot" position.
4. Hold a lighted match to the pilot and push the reset button down. Keep the button depressed for 30 seconds, and make sure that the pilot stays lighted during the entire interval.
5. Release the reset button; the pilot should keep burning.

If you cannot get the pilot lighted, there is probably something obstructing the flow of gas. Check the tiny orifice for clogging, and clean it if necessary.

If the pilot catches but goes off when you release the reset button, try holding the button down again for an additional 10 to 15 seconds. If it still fails to stay on, you either have a thermocouple that is defective or one that is not positioned properly in the flame of

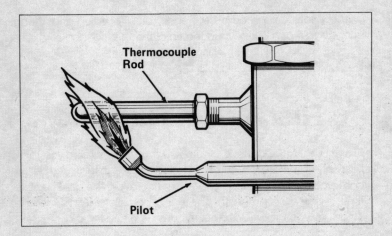

Thermocouple Rod

Pilot

the pilot. The flame from the pilot should bathe the top half inch of the thermocouple rod (the sensor tube). If it does not, loosen the bracket nuts and reposition the rod. In case you are wondering what the thermocouple does, it acts as a safety cutoff for the gas valve. When the pilot is lighted, the heat generates a slight electric current in the thermocouple that then allows gas to come from the gas valve. When the pilot goes out, the thermocouple stops sending the current, and the gas supply stops. If the thermocouple is faulty, replace it.

1. Purchase a new thermocouple of the same type, making sure that the lead-in tube is the same length as the old one.
2. Remove the bracket nut (or nuts) that hold the thermocouple unit next to the pilot.
3. Unscrew the connection nut that holds the other end of the thermocouple to the gas valve.
4. Position the tip of the new unit so that about its top ½ inch will be bathed by the pilot flame. Secure it with the bracket nut or nuts.
5. Be careful not to kink the thermocouple's lead-in tube when maneuvering the other end into position at the gas valve.
6. Turn the connection nut finger tight, and then just a quarter turn more with a wrench.
7. Relight the pilot.

The pilot flame should be steady, blue in color, and strong enough to reach out beyond the tip of the thermocouple.

55 First Aid for Furniture

YOU OFTEN SEE a piece of furniture that looks so bad you think that only complete refinishing will help it. Although that may be the case, you should do everything you can to avoid the considerable time, money, and mess involved in a complete refinishing job. Before you go the whole route, try some furniture first aid.

HERE IS WHAT YOU WILL NEED

Materials	Tools
☐ Rags	☐ Toothpicks or artist's brush
☐ Paint thinner	☐ Electric iron
☐ Fine steel wool (0000)	
☐ Lemon oil	
☐ Furniture polish	
☐ Wood stain or liquid shoe polish	
☐ Crayons or iodine diluted with denatured alcohol	
☐ Blotter	
☐ Ice cubes	

1. Clean furniture that is suffering from a severe wax build-up by rubbing it with a cloth dampened with paint thinner. Paint thinner is a great wax remover.
2. Get rid of cracking and checking in the finish by going over your furniture with four ought (0000) steel wool and lemon oil. Be careful not to rub so hard as to allow the steel wool to cut into the finish, and always rub with the grain.
3. You can often cover scratches. If they are surface scratches (just

Step 2

in the finish and not into the wood), furniture polish usually hides them. If they are down into the stain, you must replace the color. The best way is to apply some stain with a toothpick or a tiny artist's brush. You can also try liquid shoe polish, a crayon, or iodine diluted with denatured alcohol to match the color of the stain.

4. Candle wax on a table can look awful and seem impossible to remove, but a little furniture first aid should do the job. The two best approaches are: (1) Put a blotter over the drippings, and then press the blotter with a hot iron; just make sure that you move the blotter frequently so that a clean and absorbent spot is over the wax drippings at all times. (2) Hold an ice cube against the wax to make it more brittle; then just pry off the drippings.

56

Removing a Cigarette Burn from a Tabletop

UNSIGHTLY CIGARETTE BURNS on your furniture don't mean that you have to refinish the piece. Here are some tricks that you can use to hide the burns in your furniture.

HERE IS WHAT YOU WILL NEED

Materials	Tools
☐ Stain	☐ Dull rounded knife
☐ Stick shellac	☐ Clean knife
☐ Alcohol flame	
☐ Fine steel wool (0000)	
☐ Lemon oil	
☐ Clear fingernail polish	
☐ Nail polish remover	

1. The first step is to scrape away the black char. Use a dull rounded knife, and be sure to get all of the black off—even going into the wood.

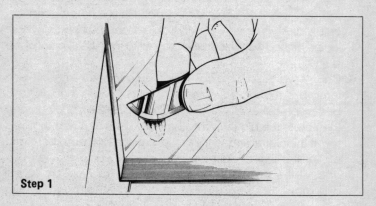

Step 1

2. If you go down into the wood on a piece that was stained, you must replace the stain. Your paint dealer should be able to help you match the color. Remember, though, that different stains react differently to different woods. One stain might give five distinctive shades when placed on five different woods.

3. With the stain back in, you are ready to fill in the gouge. Try to make it level with the rest of the table. One way is to fill the low spot with stick shellac. Stick shellac, however, is a little tricky to work with and requires some practice. You put it on by heating a knife over a alcohol flame, touching the hot knife to the stick shellac, and flowing the shellac into the indentation. You should use an alcohol flame because it does not leave sooty deposits on the knife that would mix with the shellac on your table. Flow in enough shellac to make the burned spot higher than the rest of the table. Then use a very fine abrasive (0000 steel wool) and lemon oil to cut it down even with the surface.

If you want to avoid the hassle of using stick shellac, here is another technique. Though not quite as professional in its results, it will do the job. Mix clear fingernail polish and nail polish remover about half and half, and swipe the mixture across the gouge with the polish brush. This will leave a thin coat that dries very fast. As soon as it dries, put on another coat, and keep adding coats until you build up the gouge to a point where it is level with the rest of the table. While the spot may still look a little different from the rest of the table, it will not be as unattractive as the burn was.

Removing White Spots from Furniture

57

THERE ARE ALL sorts of ways to create white rings and spots on your furniture. Setting a cold glass down without a coaster under it is one way. A hot dish left on a table without a trivet will leave a hazy spot and spilled hot coffee, alcoholic drinks, and perfume can also

cause white or hazy spots. If you thought that there was no alternative but to refinish the whole tabletop, you have some good news in
store. With an abrasive, rubbing oil, and a little elbow grease, you
can remove white spots from furniture without refinishing.

Choose a mild abrasive; four ought (0000) steel wool will do. It is
extremely fine, and unless you really bear down or use it dry, it will
not cut into the finish. You can also use such things as cigar ashes,
table salt, tooth powder, or silver polish; each is a mild abrasive. Pure
lemon oil is a great rubbing oil, but you can also use petroleum jelly,
salad oil, mayonnaise, or even paste wax.

HERE IS WHAT YOU WILL NEED

Materials	Tools
☐ Fine steel wool (0000) or another mild abrasive	☐ None
☐ Lemon oil, petroleum jelly, or other rubbing oil	
☐ Soft cloths	
☐ Furniture polish	
☐ Furniture wax	
☐ Household ammonia	

1. Put enough of the rubbing oil on to cover the white spot. If you are using a powdery abrasive, sprinkle it into the oil.
2. Using a soft cloth or the 0000 steel wool, rub in a circular fashion all around the spot. Keep it up, occasionally moving the oil away with your rag to see how well the spot is coming off.
3. When the spot is gone, take a clean cloth and remove the oily residue.
4. Polish the entire tabletop with your regular polish. If you normally use wax on the table, you will probably have to rewax the entire surface.

If you can work on alcohol stains right away, you can lift them
with a small amount of household ammonia on a soft rag. Squeeze
the rag as dry as possible, and then buff it over the stained spot
lightly.